The Palgrave Macmillan Animal Ethics Series

Series Editors

Andrew Linzey
Oxford Centre for Animal Ethics
Oxford, United Kingdom

Priscilla Cohn
Villanova, Pennsylvania, USA

Aims of the Series
In recent years, there has been a growing interest in the ethics of our treatment of animals. Philosophers have led the way, and now a range of other scholars have followed from historians to social scientists. From being a marginal issue, animals have become an emerging issue in ethics and in multidisciplinary inquiry. This series will explore the challenges that Animal Ethics poses, both conceptually and practically, to traditional understandings of human-animal relations. Specifically, the Series will:

- provide a range of key introductory and advanced texts that map out ethical positions on animals;
- publish pioneering work written by new, as well as accomplished, scholars;
- produce texts from a variety of disciplines that are multidisciplinary in character or have multidisciplinary relevance.

More information about this series at
http://www.springer.com/series/14421

Natalie Thomas

Animal Ethics and the Autonomous Animal Self

Natalie Thomas
Media Studies
University of Guelph-Humber
Toronto, Ontario, Canada

ISBN 978-1-349-93466-9   ISBN 978-1-137-58685-8 (eBook)
DOI 10.1057/978-1-137-58685-8

Library of Congress Control Number: 2016947975

© The Editor(s) (if applicable) and The Author(s) 2016
Softcover reprint of the hardcover 1st edition 2016 978-1-137-58684-1
The author(s) has/have asserted their right(s) to be identified as the author(s) of this work in accordance with the Copyright, Designs and Patents Act 1988.
This work is subject to copyright. All rights are solely and exclusively licensed by the Publisher, whether the whole or part of the material is concerned, specifically the rights of translation, reprinting, reuse of illustrations, recitation, broadcasting, reproduction on microfilms or in any other physical way, and transmission or information storage and retrieval, electronic adaptation, computer software, or by similar or dissimilar methodology now known or hereafter developed.
The use of general descriptive names, registered names, trademarks, service marks, etc. in this publication does not imply, even in the absence of a specific statement, that such names are exempt from the relevant protective laws and regulations and therefore free for general use.
The publisher, the authors and the editors are safe to assume that the advice and information in this book are believed to be true and accurate at the date of publication. Neither the publisher nor the authors or the editors give a warranty, express or implied, with respect to the material contained herein or for any errors or omissions that may have been made.

Cover image © Eureka / Alamy Stock Photo

Printed on acid-free paper

This Palgrave Macmillan imprint is published by Springer Nature
The registered company is Macmillan Publishers Ltd. London

For Achilles
with endless gratitude for opening up my heart.
And for Nigel, Timothy and Lucy, for bringing constant joy into my life.

Series Editors' Preface

This is a new book series for a new field of inquiry: Animal Ethics.

In recent years, there has been a growing interest in the ethics of our treatment of animals. Philosophers have led the way and now a range of other scholars have followed, from historians to social scientists. From being a marginal issue, animals have become an emerging issue in ethics and in multidisciplinary inquiry.

In addition, a rethink of the status of animals has been fuelled by a range of scientific investigations which have revealed the complexity of animal sentiency, cognition, and awareness. The ethical implications of this new knowledge have yet to be properly evaluated, but it is becoming clear that the old view that animals are mere things, tools, machines, or commodities cannot be sustained ethically.

But it is not only philosophy and science that are putting animals on the agenda. Increasingly, in Europe and the United States, animals are becoming a political issue as political parties vie for the green and animal votes. In turn, political scientists are beginning to look again at the history of political thought in relation to animals, and historians are beginning to revisit the political history of animal protection.

As animals grow as an issue of importance, so there have been more collaborative academic ventures leading to conference volumes, special journal issues, indeed new academic animal journals as well. Moreover, we have witnessed the growth of academic courses and university posts in Animal Ethics, Animal Welfare, Animal Rights, Animal Law, Animals and Philosophy, Human–Animal Studies, Critical Animal Studies, Animals and Society, Animals in Literature, Animals and Religion—tangible signs that a new academic discipline is emerging.

Animal Ethics is the new term for the academic exploration of the moral status of the non-human—an exploration that explicitly involves a focus on what we owe animals morally, and which also helps us to understand the influences—social, legal, cultural, religious, and political—that legitimate animal abuse. This series explores the challenges that Animal Ethics poses, both conceptually and practically, to traditional understandings of human–animal relations.

The series is needed for three reasons: (1) to provide the texts that will service the new university courses on animals; (2) to support the increasing number of students studying and academics researching in animal-related fields; and (3) because there is currently no book series that is a focus for multidisciplinary research in the field.

Specifically, the series will:

* provide a range of key introductory and advanced texts that map out ethical positions on animals;
* publish pioneering work written by new, as well as accomplished, scholars; and
* produce texts from a variety of disciplines that are multidisciplinary in character or have multidisciplinary relevance.

The new Palgrave Macmillan Series on Animal Ethics is the result of a unique partnership between Palgrave Macmillan and the Ferrater Mora Oxford Centre for Animal Ethics. The series is an integral part of the mission of the Centre to put animals on the intellectual agenda by facilitating academic research and publication. The series is also a natural complement to one of the Centre's other major projects, the *Journal of Animal Ethics*. The Centre is an independent think tank for the advancement of progressive thought about animals, and is the first Centre of its kind in the world. It aims to demonstrate rigorous intellectual enquiry and the highest standards of scholarship. It strives to be a world-class centre of academic excellence in its field.

We invite academics to visit the Centre's website www.oxfordanimalethics.com and to contact us with new book proposals for the series.

Andrew Linzey and Priscilla N. Cohn
General Editors

Acknowledgements

I would like to thank Andrew Linzey for his constant encouragement, and Patricia Marino for her support and feedback in all the stages of this work. I would also like to thank the Department of Philosophy at the University of Waterloo, and its members, for providing advice and criticisms on the content of this book in its various forms, and for allowing me to present the ideas here in multiple colloquia. I am also appreciative of the support from the University of Guelph-Humber, specifically Jerry Chomyn, whose enthusiasm for my research and writing outside the department seems limitless.

I am also deeply grateful to my parents, who taught me at a very young age to love and respect all the members of our family, including the dogs and cats we shared a home with. Thanks to them, I always consider living with animals as a necessary part of my life, and over the years I have had the privilege of learning from and sharing my own home with dogs and cats from various origins. I am thankful for the inspiration and knowledge I gained from Roxie, a Rottweiler and German Shepherd dog who was saved from the home of an animal hoarder, and with whom I shared so many of her first experiences in life outside a cage. She showed me the harm and suffering caused by an inability to see her as an autonomous individual who had her own needs, desires, and preferences, just as humans do. Thanks to the Guelph Humane Society I was able to spend a few invaluable years with Roxie, and their continued work in the community to protect and rehome animals is a source of hope and faith in the ability of humans to be compassionate and effective in alleviating animal suffering.

Finally, I am grateful to all those who study animals and their minds without harming them in the process. The intellectual curiosity and caring attitudes that motivate such scientists and philosophers are crucial to the pursuit of improving our ethical relations with animals. I have encountered many people that have changed their own attitudes towards animals based on revelations about how animals think and feel, and so this research is indispensable to the bigger project of challenging societal perceptions of animals as merely a means to our own ends. In particular, I want to thank Bernard Rollin and Marc Bekoff, who are examples of such people, and who both gave of their own time to discuss with me the ideas and arguments presented in this book.

Contents

1 Introduction   1

2 Animals as Agents   7

3 Self-Awareness and Selfhood in Animals   37

4 Autonomy and Animals   69

5 Other Views of Animal Ethics   97

6 Kantian Ethics and Animals   129

7 Conclusions and Further Directions   155

Bibliography   163

Index   171

1

Introduction

Despite an increasing awareness of the welfare of animals, and an evolving interest in animal minds, animals are still treated, by and large, merely as resources for human use. Practices involving animals—such as factory farming, entertainment, and experimentation—demonstrate a general view of animals as objects, rather than as subjective individuals who have awareness of themselves and of their own experiences. On the one hand, it is fairly easy to recognize another self when we interact with dogs, cats, or other companion animals. Most people would not deny that their dog or cat is someone, rather than just something. This is because there seems to be something unique to interacting with another creature that has a mind, and we are able to recognize that individual as someone that shares certain traits with us. Dan Zahavi (2005), in his examination of selfhood, writes, "What must be realized is that bodies of others differ radically from inanimate objects, and that our perception of these minded bodies is unlike our ordinary perception of objects." (155). For him, the experience we have when we interact with another is distinctive as we experience behaviour as an expression of a mind. This is what allows for empathy, where we are able to feel or imagine our way into the experiences of others, and which motivates us to treat them with moral consideration and care. But even when we do treat certain animals with care and consideration, we tend to turn away from and dismiss the cruel treatment of other animals from a failure to acknowledge inconsistencies in our own beliefs and actions. Unfortunately, we cannot rely on our emotions to consistently guide us towards the ethical treatment of all animals, as emotional connections are based mainly on direct encounters with others. This means that we need also to take into consideration rational reasons for believing that most animals are in fact self-aware, without relying solely on experience or emotion for such beliefs.

Our reluctance to take the moral consideration of animals seriously and consistently suggests that we view animal ethics as optional, and dependent upon our own changing needs and desires. As a philosopher, I believe that being as consistent as possible in our beliefs is important in pursuing true knowledge; as an ethicist, I believe that this can lead us and others, both human and animal, to living better and happier lives. To achieve greater consistency in our ethical decisions and actions we need to consider on what rational grounds an individual is owed direct moral consideration. This means identifying which traits or characteristics of individuals are morally relevant, and then determining which individuals possess these morally relevant features. Many theories of animal ethics adopt this method, by looking at whether or not animals possess certain capacities that make them morally considerable, and I follow this trend to a certain extent. I too ask the same fundamental questions as other ethical theorists, such as "Do we owe animals direct moral consideration, and if so, on what grounds?" and "To what extent do we owe animals direct moral consideration?" However, I believe that many of these other theories have overlooked the importance of certain key features of what makes individuals morally considerable and valuable. These features are agency, self-awareness, and autonomy. My main claim in this book is that many, if not most, animals are self-aware, autonomous agents. Certainly, these capacities and characteristics are included in various ways in some of the most well known theories of animal ethics, but they are left as secondary considerations to the issues of rights, the ability to suffer, and the weighing of or equal consideration of interests. These views tend to fall into distinct categories that are labelled as rights views, abolitionist views, and welfarist views. Whereas welfarist views take animal suffering and its alleviation into consideration, they do not always succeed in treating animal suffering in morally consistent ways, and they are sometimes overly cautious in ascribing animals morally relevant traits that would dramatically change our relationships with them. This is sometimes due to fears of incorrectly anthropomorphizing the behaviours of animals, and sometimes as a result of a hesitation to call animals conscious or self-aware.

The rights views take more than just animal suffering into consideration, but can have difficulty in resolving conflicts between different rights holders, especially when it comes to those between humans and other animals. Also, ascribing rights to a particular group does not necessarily guarantee that they are treated in morally acceptable ways.

Abolitionist views demand the complete cessation of all relationships that involve the use of animals for human purposes, sometimes including relationships that can, in fact, be beneficial for both species involved, such as the relationships between humans and companion animals. For these reasons, I believe that the right way to treat animals does not entail any one of these particular views, but rather that we avoid using animals *merely* as a means to our own ends. That we ought to treat animals as intentional agents that are self-aware and autonomous is the view that I present and defend in this book, as an alternative to other views of animal ethics that focus on different morally relevant capacities of individuals as the grounds for moral consideration. To support this view, I provide an overview of current arguments and evidence for animal agency and self-awareness, as well as a conceptual analysis of autonomy as the grounds for direct moral duties towards animals. It is my hope that the ambiguities surrounding the definitions of these capacities and concepts can be clarified here, for the benefit of both the reader, and for those that use these concepts in their work on research into animal minds and ethics.

The book is divided into seven chapters. In Chap. 2, I argue for a conception of agency in animals that admits to degrees among individuals and across species. Included in this chapter is an overview of arguments supporting the claims that some animals can properly be said to possess beliefs, desires, and preferences. Based on these arguments, I claim that animals can also be more or less rational, in terms of being able to make decisions and direct their actions based on reasons. An animal can be considered minimally rational, and this is enough to say that some animals can be considered agents. If we grant that some animals are intentional agents, then further questions arise as to whether or not animals can also be considered as moral agents, or individuals who are able to act for moral reasons. In examining views that claim animals are minimal moral agents, or moral subjects, the idea that animals are acting agents is further supported. Although it is generally accepted that animals have minds and are able to perceive others and objects within their surrounding environments, there are still sceptics who would deny either that animals do not possess concepts or that, even if they do, we are unable to know anything about them. But, to investigate animal minds at all, some basic assumptions are needed, and whether or not these assumptions are warranted is the focus of this chapter.

In Chap. 3, I claim that some animals are self-aware, to varying degrees. To do this requires an examination of the various ways self-awareness has been defined and understood, and so I provide an account of some of the main views that support the idea that self-awareness can be more or less complex, depending on other mental capacities an animal might also possess. From a basic sense of mine-ness, body-ness, or phenomenal awareness, to a fully-fledged, reflective self-identity, self-awareness is a trait that most conscious individuals possess, including many animals. The view of self-awareness as existing on a gradient of complexity is also supported through an overview of empirical research on animal minds, which shows that—while there is no one specific mental capacity that can be used to definitively argue that some animals are self-aware—there is a growing amount of evidence to support the claim that self-awareness can be indicated by some of these capacities, such as tool use and communication. By arguing that some animals are minimally self-aware, I believe this provides the grounds for their moral consideration, as creatures for which experiences can be good or bad, and so I also examine ways that even a minimal sense of self-awareness in others can obligate us towards them, morally.

If many animals can be understood to be self-aware, then it changes our view of them as merely objects for our use, to seeing them as individual selves deserving of moral consideration. In ethics it is assumed that we only have direct moral obligations towards other selves, and not towards inanimate objects. Although this distinction seems straightforward and non-controversial, the widespread treatment of animals as objects to be used as a means to human ends speaks otherwise. And so, in Chap. 4, I examine the concept of autonomy as it applies to individuals who are self-aware agents, and as the grounds for owing others direct moral obligations. If acting agents are self-aware, however minimally, and able to direct their own actions towards achieving certain goals or fulfilling their own interests, then we owe such individuals respect for that freedom. I argue that autonomy, if understood as the ability to act freely and for one's own reasons, exists at both minimal and rich levels in animals and humans, depending on the complexity of mental capacities that different individuals possess. Respecting the autonomy of animals requires us to invest time and energy to better identify those features of individuals that indicate how we ought to treat them and, as the focus is on individual animals, it also means that we cannot assume that all animals of one species ought to be treated in the same ways. By presenting a view of autonomy that admits to degrees, rather than as a feature that is either possessed by individuals or not, I believe that we have a stronger basis for an animal ethics than those that focus only on the capacity for suffering, or on the consideration of comparative interests.

There are some established theories in animal ethics that have served to extend moral consideration towards animals based on various capacities that both animals and humans have in common. In Chap. 5, I consider some of these views, including those held by Peter Singer, Tom Regan, and Bernard Rollin. I also consider a view held by Lori Gruen that challenges this approach to animal ethics and focuses instead on the importance of difference, care, and empathy as the sources of our moral obligations towards animals. The contributions these philosophers have made, and continue to make to the field of animal ethics, are invaluable, as they all aim to expose many human–animal interactions as unethical based on the use of reason and emotion. The purpose of this chapter then, is not to argue that these theories are wholly inaccurate, but rather to show that by omitting a thorough consideration of self-awareness and autonomy they suffer from problems in both theory and application. And so, after explaining the nature of some of these problems, I present reasons why the inclusion of the self-awareness and autonomy of animals is required as a more accurate ground for animal ethics. Indeed, I believe that these theories can work in conjunction with each other, and with my own view, by acknowledging and incorporating these concepts into their own theories.

In Chap. 6, I examine Kantian moral theory and its application to animals. Although Kant himself did not believe that animals are autonomous, or that we have direct moral obligations towards them, he did not entirely discount them from moral consideration. Some recent reinterpretations of his arguments show that it is possible to support the claim that animals are ends-in-themselves, and are worthy of direct moral consideration. As autonomy is a central concept in Kantian moral theory, I consider how these views might support my own by challenging traditional Kantian notions of rationality and what it means to be an autonomous individual. I argue that animals can be considered autonomous ends-in-themselves and that Kantian moral theory can be seen to support this claim, along with being a source of guidance for our ethical treatment of animals. I then conclude the book with further considerations of what problems still remain in the study of animal ethics, and in what direction further research should continue.

It is important to clarify here that throughout the book I refer to non-human animals simply as animals. This is for the sake of brevity only, and it is not meant to obscure the fact that humans are also animals, or that there are differences between individual animals or animal species. As much of what I am arguing for is focused on the mental capacities of animals, it is also important to note that much of the research into animal minds is based on studies that include mammals, birds, and sometimes fish. Drawing any sort of line between minded or non-minded, conscious or non-conscious animals is very difficult, and I leave that purposively ambiguous in this book. If we are unsure, or have some reason to believe that certain individuals or species should also be considered conscious, then it is best to include them in the realm of moral consideration rather than risk an arbitrary exclusion.

Reference

Zahavi, D. (2005). *Subjectivity and selfhood: Investigating the first-person perspective*. Cambridge: The MIT Press.

2
Animals as Agents

Introduction

People enjoy watching animals. Whether it is watching dogs play in the park, or birds gathering at a feeder, we are fascinated by the actions of animals, both wild and domesticated. Part of this is wonder, especially when we observe animals acting in ways that seem so similar to ours. We may question why certain animals act in the specific ways that they do, and we might compare them to our own to try to determine the reasons. None of this kind of thinking seems particularly scientific or philosophical. But if we take the question of what animals are thinking seriously, it quickly leads us into the realms of science, psychology, biology, ethics, and philosophy.

One way to begin the investigation into animal minds is to consider the concept of agency, and what makes someone an acting agent, rather than, for example, a passive object. If animals are agents, then they are capable of making choices, and this means that we owe them moral obligations since we generally consider that those who can make choices possess a will. Having a will means that the creature in question is not a mere object, but someone who values the freedom to make choices based on beliefs, desires, and preferences. As I argue further in subsequent chapters, being an acting and self-aware agent is the basis of autonomy, and so provides the grounds for moral consideration. In this chapter I provide an account of agency, along with beliefs, desires, preferences, intentions, and rationality to argue that animals are practical agents in more or less complex ways. This includes a consideration of the cognitive features required for agency, and what it takes to be considered an agent that acts on the basis of reasons. I argue that most animals can be considered minimal agents, based on evidence provided by arguments and assumptions that make sense of observable animal behaviours. In fact, it is important to remember that the study of animal cognition relies on the assumption that animals are agents, even if only minimally so. This is because, as Kristin Andrews (2012) suggests, animals would not be the proper subjects of cognitive studies if animals did not have beliefs. As all cognitive systems have beliefs, then animals must have beliefs. This similarly applies to the idea that animals are agents. For if animal behaviours are not caused by propositional attitudes, and if all cognitive systems are agents, then animals could not possibly be agents. So, as it is widely accepted among cognitive scientists that animals are proper subjects of study, it is also widely accepted that animals have beliefs and can act intentionally. While there is not unanimous agreement among scientists in general that animals are agents, I agree with the suggestion that it is the job of the philosopher to "distinguish more clearly among different features of animal cognition" (Allen and Bekoff 2007, pp. 301–302) to differentiate which mental capacities should be used to ground ethical arguments about animals.

Agency

Are animals agents? Discussions of agency are generally complicated by the lack of agreement on two issues. First, there are various answers to the question of what agency is, with definitions based on the full range of basic biological or neurological to fully-fledged reflective rationality. Second, there are an abundance of answers to the question of which specific cognitive features constitute agency, and these are based on the definition provided in response to the first issue. Without providing a detailed overview of the various definitions and descriptions of agency, there is some agreement that, whether or not we are talking about biological or fully rational agency, what is relevant here is the general ability to control one's own actions, or to act intentionally. There is also a general consensus that an agent can be more or less aware of and/or more or less able to rationally or reflectively evaluate their own reasons for acting. Lilian O'Brien (2015) discusses this idea when pointing out that the ability to make choices is often associated with having a will. Having a will, she says, on some views, is generally associated with other things like having desires, the capacity for deliberation and making decisions, and the capacity to have control over one's movements to execute a decision. She also points out that agents can be more or less sophisticated in their actions, where more sophisticated agents seem able to reflect on their desires. In other words, while all agents are able to initiate their own actions, there are degrees to which an agent can rationally or reflectively evaluate their own actions. I believe that all agents act for reasons, but that there is a distinction between individuals who are minimally rational and those who are more fully rational when it comes to evaluating their own reasons for acting. The main point here is that "At the heart of rational practical agency is control and it is surely a defining feature of intentional action that it is a movement or bodily state that is under some kind of control by the agent." (O'Brien 2015, p. 6). Animals, then, can be seen as practical agents who control their own movements based on reasons, however minimal they might seem.

Motivation for an agent to act is based on beliefs, desires, goals, and preferences. Without these features, we would lack any explanation for the causes that initiate actions. In the following sections, I examine each of these features individually to see whether or not we can reasonably ascribe them to animals. However, it is important to note here that agents have degrees of self-awareness that are relevant to those beliefs, experiences, and perceptions that give rise to intentional actions. Without even a most minimal sense of self, an individual could not distinguish between oneself and the surrounding environment, and so could not have preferences or desires to achieve certain goals. Although here I am arguing that some animals possess the relevant features that constitute agents, and so should be considered intentional agents, I argue in Chap. 3 that most animals also possess self-awareness. It is by virtue of being self-aware agents that animals are autonomous and are deserving of direct moral obligations, as I argue in Chap. 4.

Beliefs, Desires, Preferences, and Intentions

Before we can discuss whether or not animals can be said to have beliefs, desires, and preferences, it is worth noting the underlying assumptions within the field of experimental psychology known as cognitivism. This is important as this view rejected the previous methodology and ideology of behaviourism that denied the existence of mental states in animals, such as beliefs and desires, in favour of focusing exclusively on external and observable behaviours and the conditions under which they were elicited. Cognitivists assume that people and some animals have minds (Dennett 1995, p. 111).

Arguments in favour of animals having minds tend to take two main forms and, according to Kristin Andrews (2012), these are: the argument from analogy; and the inference to the best explanation. The argument from analogy takes the following form:

1. All animals I already know to have a mind (i.e. humans) have property x.
2. Individuals of species y have property x.
3. Therefore, individuals of species y probably have a mind. (Andrews 2012)

The inference to the best explanation argument is another way to reach the same conclusion:

1. Individuals of species x engage in behaviours y.
2. The best scientific explanation for an individual engaging in behaviours y is that it has a mind.
3. Therefore, it is likely that individuals of species x have minds. (Andrews 2012)

2 Animals as Agents

Despite some debate as to what is meant by animals having minds, just as there is debate concerning the nature of consciousness itself, these two arguments provide a reasonable foundation for the study of animal cognition. For without first accepting that animals have minds, there would be no reason to investigate whether or not animals have beliefs, desires, or preferences. As a result, any attempt to understand why an animal behaves or acts in a certain way would be fairly futile. As the assumption that animals have minds helps to anticipate and explain their behaviours, just as it does with humans, then it explains why there is such widespread agreement that animals have minds. Of course, with any area of study, there are sceptics who challenge some of these basic assumptions. For example, some might argue that we need a more precise account of what a mind actually is, or how it is that we can be certain about our knowledge of the content of other minds. These are examples of areas where science and philosophy can depart from each other. As philosophers spend considerable time analyzing such concepts and debating their meanings, scientists must rely on certain assumptions to move forward with research. Marc Bekoff (2006a), himself a scientist, warns against having too much scepticism and too little common sense when it comes to studying animal minds. He writes,

> The minds and feelings of individuals other than oneself are private. Access is limited because we can't really get into the head or heart of another being. Sceptics often use this solipsistic line of reasoning, but it really can be a dead end when practical matters are of primary concern. Of course other minds are private, but that doesn't stop us trying to understand what another human is thinking or feeling or stop us using this information to make future compassionate decisions. (2006a, p. 33)

He continues by pointing out that, often, sceptics demand a higher level of evidence and proof for the existence of animal emotions and their subjective experiences than for humans. This sceptical view lacks justification given that studies in animal behaviour can make accurate predictions without having to know everything or have absolute certainty about their knowledge. And so, for the purposes of this book, I want simply to claim that we have sufficient support to argue that animals are minded creatures, based on the reasons presented above. As such, they are legitimate and proper subjects of cognitive studies, and must possess cognitive capacities of various kinds.

Taking these assumptions seriously means that any creature that has a mind can also be assumed to possess the cognitive features that constitute agency. This is because, as Daniel Dennett (1995) puts it, "Cognitivists… take the mind seriously, and develop theories, models, explanations, that invoke, as real items, these internal, mental goings-on. People (at least some other animals) have minds after all—they are *rational agents*." (p. 111). For Dennett, having a mind is what it means to be an agent. By accepting that animals are minded, and that mental contents are real items in the world, then we can study the extent to which animals act intentionally. That is, if rational agents are able to act for reasons, however simple those reasons might be, then they are also able to act intentionally, in more or less complex ways, depending on the relative complexity of the mental capacities possessed by individual animals.

To say that animals have minds is to say that they think, and this means that there must be thoughts and mental contents within those minds. In other words, to say an animal thinks means that we are ascribing beliefs and desires to the minds of animals. This seems in some ways very straightforward, as we assume an animal knows certain things, like "the food is in my bowl" or "the squirrel is in the tree". Beliefs are, in their most simple forms, internal representations of perceived qualities of the world. Common sense tells us that animals must have beliefs to act in the ways that they do, or that their actions are a result of their mental representations of the world around them and of their own beliefs about how to direct their actions in order to fulfill their desires or preferences. However, doubts have been raised in relation to this notion that animals possess beliefs and desires, and I want to examine these briefly, along with some of the main responses to these views, to argue that many animals are indeed minded, and that they do act, based on their own beliefs and desires, as practical, intentional agents.

The problem that is often raised in relation to animal beliefs revolves around the identity of the content of those beliefs (Rowlands 2012, p. 44; Andrews 2015, p. 85). What exactly an animal is thinking when, for example, it chases a squirrel up a tree, is difficult for us to surmise as observers of this behaviour. It is clear that there is some notion, for the dog, that there is a squirrel in the tree, but some have argued that without an understanding that the squirrel is a mammal, has a skeleton, and so on, then it does possess a concept of a squirrel in the same way that we do. As all these beliefs are part of what constitutes the concept of a squirrel, and as the dog does not have them, then it is argued that the ascription of the belief that a squirrel is in the tree is problematic. This sort of view on the ascription of beliefs is called attribution-holism as it means that beliefs can only be ascribed to those who share our belief network. If animals do not share in this belief network, then they do not have beliefs (Rowlands 2012, p. 46). Another simpler way of characterizing this sort of argument, and removing the attribution-holism requirement, would look like this, according to Andrews (2015):

1. We cannot say what animals think.
2. If we cannot say what animals think, then they do not have beliefs.
3. Therefore animals do not have beliefs. (87)

The idea here is that if we are unable to actually say what it is that an animal believes, then we are not warranted in saying that the animal believes in anything. Additionally, without humans and animals sharing a common language or common concepts, we could be left with the impossibility of ever being able to understand how animals represent objects in the world. This poses a challenge for explaining why animals act, which in turn undermines the claim that animals are intentional agents. If they do not possess beliefs or concepts about the world around them, then how can they direct their actions or act on the basis of reasons? For this reason, it is worth examining some of the strongest replies to these concerns about animal beliefs.

Colin Allen (1999, 2013) addresses the problem of concept ascription to animals using two different approaches. Or perhaps more accurately, he responds to two different aspects of the same broader problem. For while it may be impossible to know exactly what an animal's concepts are, or exactly what they are like, it is unjustifiable to argue that we do not know whether animals have concepts at all. Just because humans can express mental concepts through the use of words does not mean that those who lack language do not have concepts themselves. Allen (2013) responds to the concern that language is required for concept formation by pointing out that words only approximate mental concepts and their associated cognitive states, which are, most likely, constantly changing. Belief attributions, as they are made in language, are imprecise both for humans and for animals. However, this imprecision does not negate the use of attributions but rather shows the need for a method to determine the accuracy of an attribution, in terms of its relevance or similarity, to the subject's cognitive state (Andrews 2015, p. 88). Allen posits an analogy between the abstractions that can be made from geometric objects and the attribution of beliefs to cognitive systems by pointing out that when rules of transformation are applied to geometric objects to reduce them to less precise objects, the resulting properties are commensurate with the original objects. In other words, the object can be transformed while preserving its overall structure, and this allows for the stating of similarities across different contexts of comparison. He argues that cognitive systems are multidimensional objects (like geometric objects), and that attributing intentional states to them is "akin to abstraction by dimensional reduction (analogues to projection and slicing), deliberate downgrading of precision (blurring), and other ways of describing invariant aspects of the systems" (Allen 2013, p. 254). Allen acknowledges and responds to potential problems with this model and analogy, but the strength of his views lies in the idea that two different cognitive systems can be thinking the same thing if we abstract the original representations from them. This means that although animals and humans may have different associations or contexts for similar mental concepts, we have good reason to make mental state attributions to both, even if these are imprecise. Allen offers an example that, in his view, to say that he and his dog both see that there is a squirrel in the garden "is to take two rather different shapes in initial spaces of different dimensionality and then to squash them down to a single representation whose major axis line ups with certain features in the world" (2013, p. 258). In this way we are justified in making concept attributions to animals as well as humans (like children) who lack language and the ability to express their concepts in words.

The more general problem of ascribing beliefs to animals, given the previous discussion on whether or not animals represent the world in the form of concepts, is also addressed by Allen who provides a framework for arguing that it is reasonable to ascribe concepts to animal minds. He does this by presenting the following conditions under which it is reasonable to believe that an animal possesses a concept of an object:

1. O systematically discriminates some Xs from some non-Xs; and
2. O is capable of detecting some of its own discrimination errors between Xs and non-Xs; and
3. O is capable of learning to better discriminate Xs from non-Xs as a consequence of its capacity (2). (1999, p. 37)

These conditions do not provide an understanding of what it is for an animal to possess a concept, but it does provide us with reasonable grounds for attributing a concept to an animal at all. Allen provides evidence in the form of animal studies to show how the capacities required for the three conditions seem to exist in various species. For Allen, "the internal states implicated in the explanation of these capacities are worthy of being designated as concepts" (1999, p. 39). What this shows is that for animals to use these capacities indicates that there are internal states of representation of the world that are separate from perceptual representations at any given moment in time. These internal representations that are separate from immediate perceptual information must be mental concepts for us to make sense of their ability to discriminate among objects and to recognize mistakes in discrimination. This allows us to explain animal behaviour in terms of intentionality, as we can track the content of animal beliefs, regardless of whether or not the animal itself is capable of entertaining the content of its own thoughts. Mark Rowlands (2012) presents this strategy of being able to explain an animal's reasons for acting so that we can make accurate predictions of an animal's behaviour, thereby addressing the problem created by trying to ascribe content to animals which is only appropriate to humans. That is, according to this view:

> A propositional content, p, can therefore be employed as a way of explaining the behavior of an animal, even if p is not a content the animal entertains, or is even capable of entertaining, to the extent that p tracks a distinct

propositional content, p^*, that can, in fact, be attributed to that animal. Of course, since in the absence of extensive empirical investigation, we cannot be sure of the identity of p^*, p constitutes, in effect, our best guess as to the proposition that will track the propositional content we think we can legitimately ascribe to the animal. (Rowlands 2012, p. 58)

Rowlands believes that by ascribing beliefs to an animal relative to context, we can avoid the problem of making content ascriptions to animals that are appropriate to humans. For example, our concept of a squirrel is anchored to humans by virtue of our network of beliefs, whereas a dog's concept of squirrel is anchored to its own context. When human concepts of squirrel and tree are accurately connected to the dog's (context) concept of squirrel and tree then the truth of the ascription "there is a squirrel in the tree" to the dog guarantees the truth of "there is a squirrel in the tree". (Andrews 2015, pp. 88–89) Rowlands' argument provides us with a way to legitimize the ascription of beliefs to animals, and it overcomes the problems raised by sceptics about not being able to know what animals think, as well as concerns about the role language plays in concept formation. Although there have been numerous responses to these problems, the view presented here is important as it both legitimizes the study of animal minds and thought and provides a practical means for interpreting animal behaviour. It also lends support for the notion that animal minds and thoughts can be more or less complex, in terms of concepts and representations of the world around them. As I argue in Chap. 4, this has important implications for the treatment of animals when the relationship between agency and autonomy is examined.

Rationality

A constitutive feature of agency is rationality. A very commonly cited "gap" between humans and other animals is the ability to reason, where humans are considered to be the sole possessors of this mental capacity. However, reason can mean or refer to different things, and one can clearly be more or less able to reason. Kristin Andrews (2015) notes that there are well-supported views that posit different systems of reasoning, and different gradations of reasoning that apply to both humans and other animals, and that, ultimately, these are "questions for further research" (104). For my purposes, the relevant question here is whether or not animals can be said to be at least minimally rational and, if so, whether this further supports the notion that animals can be agents? The intellectually disabled and small children are examples of humans whose ability to reason is diminished, and yet we would still treat them and view them as agents, capable of directing their own behaviours and actions. In a similar way, animals can be more or less rational, and here I take reason to refer to the ability to make choices or act for reasons, whether good or bad ones, evaluated or not. If animals do act for reasons, based on their beliefs, desires, and preferences, then they are acting rationally, and thus are intentional agents, even if, in some cases, only minimally so. I take the view that the difference between humans and other animals, in terms of rationality, is then a matter of degree, rather than one of the possession or exclusion of rationality altogether. This view seems the most plausible given the evidence and arguments that have been made for and against the existence in animals of the ability to reason.

Fred Dretske (2006) makes some significant distinctions between the kinds or levels of rationality that exist in both humans and animals, and argues that (some) animals are minimally rational, as opposed to biologically or fully rational. Biological rationality, according to Dretske, is something like our blink reflex, where the action is not purposeful, but can be understood as designed by natural selection to achieve greater fitness. This is because biological rationality is not governed by thought (2006, p. 107). Dretske argues that minimal rationality differs from biological rationality, as "Minimal rationality requires that what is done be done for reasons, but it doesn't require that it be done for good reasons. Nor does it require reasoning. Although the behaviour must be explained by a thought in order to qualify as minimally rational, it needn't be rationalized or rationally justified by the thought that explains it, and the agent needn't have computed (reasoned) his way to that result." (2006, p. 108). Dretske believes that it is useful to assume that animals act for reasons based on thought, as it allows us to separate the question of having good reasons (for acting) from having reasons at all. As we tend to judge reason on the basis of having good reasons, we can tend to ignore reason as the cause of behaviours that we cannot, at first glance, understand. Once again, this argument supports the intentional stance by making the assumption that animals act as a result of reasons, and therefore are intentional agents. Without this first assumption, we could not even begin to investigate what reasons an animal has for its behaviour, thus making it impossible to understand animal behaviour at all. Further to this, Dretske also argues, similarly to Eric Saidel (2009), that learning is integral to distinguishing minimally rational actions from mechanistic ones. Referring to cases where birds learn not to eat monarch butterflies, or any butterflies that look similar to monarchs, as a result of becoming ill, Dretske argues that is must be thought that allows birds to engage in this avoidance behaviour. Some kind of internal mental representation in the bird's mind of these butterflies explains the cause of the resulting behaviour. Dretske concludes:

> Is the bird's behaviour really purposeful? Does the bird really *think* (mistakenly) that the bug it sees tastes bad? Is this really why it avoids the bug? All I have argued, I know, is that in this kind of learning process an internal state that indicates or means something about the animal's external environment comes to play a role in the animal's subsequent behaviour, and it comes to play that role because of what it means…The informational content or meaning of this internal, caused element is, thus, genuinely explanatory. This, I concede, is not sufficient to show that *thought* is governing the acquired behaviour in the relevant (explanatory) sense since I have not shown that internal states with meaning of this kind are thoughts. Still, we have here, if not thought itself, a plausible antecedent of thought—an internal representation whose meaning or content explains why the system in which it occurs behaves the way it does…To my ear, that sounds enough like thought not to haggle about what is still missing. (2006, pp. 114–115)

As we encountered with the concepts of agency and belief, the wide variety of definitions of rationality and thought make it difficult to reach one certain concept of each. But if we can explain an animal's behaviour by identifying the possible reasons and mental representations that cause them, then we can at least agree that, regardless of the specific nature of such representations, assuming them is the best way to explain and predict that behaviour. When studying animal behaviour, researchers look for capabilities that may be associated with reason, such as tool use and problem-solving skills. Tool use by animals is best explained, for example, as the ability to identify a problem, consider various ways of solving it, and understanding how objects can be used to overcome the problem (Andrews 2012). This sort of thing would be a good example of minimal rationality, for Dretske, as it involves the kind of learning process that he describes as requiring an internal representation whose content explains why the animal acts the way it does.

Rationality, as the ability to act for reasons, is required for one to be considered an agent. These reasons are constituted by, and best explained as, a result of the possession of beliefs, desires, and preferences. Some animals can be considered minimally rational and able to direct their own actions and behaviours based on internal mental representations. Although some would argue that even minimal forms of rationality require a linguistic capability, it is reasonable to argue that non-linguistic forms of reasoning are employed by animals to make decisions. Hans-Johann Glock (2013) highlights the problem by saying that it would seem that "I-thoughts", or self-consciousness, required for animal reasoning might imply the need for language, as when an animal engages in practical reasoning. This is because if an animal thinks about how to bring about a certain state of affairs, they will reason in a way that goes something like, "If I P, then X, so I'll P" (Glock 2013, p. 136). Glock argues that there are forms of self-awareness that do not require language, such that an animal can be aware of its own actions and consequences without having an explicit sense of self, or a consciousness of its own mental phenomena. He believes that simple self-awareness is implied by the idea of intentional action itself, as "behaviour can only be explained by reference to reasons if it is under the control of the agent, and such control clearly presupposes awareness of what one is doing" (Glock 2013, p. 136). From this, Glock further argues that animals may be capable of rudimentary forms of practical reasoning, which simply means that they are able to assess alternatives and choose in a deliberate way, which means their choice is controlled and responsive to the situation they are in. This means that "Complex non-linguistic creatures can weigh the conflicting claims of objective features of the situation, including their own behaviour, and act accordingly. As mentioned before, they can also have and adopt purposes or goals, that is the ends for the sake of which they act." (Glock 2013, p. 137) As a result of this capacity for minimal reasoning, Glock claims that we owe animals moral consideration, as it means that animals are agents, capable of acting for reasons and, as such, we ought to respect the ability to make free choices. We take it as morally wrong to frustrate the preferences of choices of others, including humans and animals. Although Glock takes a different stance to mine on the moral implications of such a view on the mental capacities of animals, his arguments do show that the differences between humans and other animals is a matter of degree, and not of kind, in terms of beliefs, agency, rationality, and choice.

So, minimal rationality is a feature of agency as it allows for the ability to make choices based on preferences, beliefs, and desires, and we ought to respect that agency as it implies the possession of a will and freedom of choice.

Intentionality

For animals to be considered agents, they must be able to act intentionally. Intentional action is motivated by beliefs that are based on representations of the world and the surrounding environment, and when we ask someone why they acted as they did, we expect to be given reasons for their actions. Although we are sometimes at a loss to explain our own actions, we do not doubt that we had reasons for acting. We can, however, put our reasons into words, whereas animals cannot. How then can we be justified in making the assumption that animals act intentionally, and not just as a result of instinct or a behavioural response to environmental stimuli? Can animals direct their actions intentionally, based on beliefs?

One way to make sense of animal actions is to adopt the intentional stance towards them, based on Daniel Dennett's view. Dennett (2012) provides an argument that adopts the terms of folk psychology to answer questions about when we are justified in attributing minds to others. When we assume the intentional stance towards something, we are claiming that "anything that is usefully and voluminously predictable from the intentional stance is, by definition, an intentional system" (Dennett 2012, p. 1). When we apply folk psychology to animals, we are accepting the assumption that animals (or at least some of them) are minimally rational in the sense that they have beliefs based on their perceptions and can act on those beliefs to satisfy their desires and achieve their goals. Taking the intentional stance towards animals means that for an animal to be an intentional agent its behaviours are explained and predicted by ascribing beliefs, desires, and preferences to them. Actions by agents are governed by the rational consideration of their beliefs and desires. As Dennett explains "the intentional stance is the strategy of interpreting the behaviour of an entity (person, animal, artefact, whatever) by treating it as if it were a rational agent who governed by its 'choice' of 'action' by a 'consideration' of its 'beliefs' and 'desires'" (2012, p. 1). Despite the difficulties of agreeing on the term belief, Dennett argues that it is simply whatever information guides an agent's actions. The best explanation for animals having beliefs is that their behaviour can best be explained and predicted by assuming that this is true. Very simply, we can observe animals, watch what they notice, and figure out what they want through interpreting their behaviours, which allows us to explain and predict their actions. The intentional stance is a valuable tool because it works. The "reality" of beliefs is irrelevant to the usefulness of assuming that (some) animals are intentional agents (Dennett 2012, p. 2).

There is, however, a potential problem with Dennett's view when we want to say that animals act intentionally in ways that are different from non-mental objects, like plants or machines. For, in his view, any object that can be said to have a "goal" can be described using intentional language and can be ascribed beliefs and desires to explain its behaviour. This is where the role of reason makes an important difference in any account of intentionality. For an agent to act on the basis of reasons, however simple they may be, rationality is required. This means that only agents who *genuinely* possess beliefs and desires and who act on their contents with the aim of achieving certain goals can truly be called intentional. Mark Okrent (2007) calls this instrumental rationality, and he argues that humans and some animals are properly called intentional agents when they are able to act on the basis of reasons which can be explained by the contents of the relevant beliefs and desires and how they are used to achieve certain goals. Okrent explains that, for an agent to act intentionally, the content of her desire is what fixes the goal of her action, while the content of the belief fixes what the agent actually does to satisfy her desire. What the agent does is not simply a function of her desires and her environment (like it is for those who lack instrumental rationality), but rather what action is taken is a function of both what she desires and what she believes (Okrent 2007, p. 109). In this way, the reasons for an agent to act are the bases of intentional behaviours, and only those with mental states that allow an organism to rationalize or justify their acts can be considered instrumentally rational. This means that in cases where an organism's behaviours can be explained without appealing to reasons, while they can still be described as intentional, they are not rational. As Okrent explains it:

> The difference between those agents that act in order to achieve goals and have intentional states with content and those agents that act to achieve goals and lack such states is the difference between those agents that act in an instrumentally rational fashion and those that don't. Only agents that act rationally have reasons of their own for what they do. And only agents that have such reasons act as they do because of the intentional contents of their beliefs and desires. We can only know an agent has intentional states with contents only if that agent acts as she does because of the contents of those intentional states. So our knowledge of the intentional states of agents derives entirely from our understanding of the agents' behavior as rational. (2007, p. 111)

This view of rationality and its relation to intentional behaviour allows for the idea that reason comes in degrees, where some animals, both at the individual and species levels, can be more or less rational. The key to rationality, according to Okrent, is the ability to learn new behaviours or actions that help an animal to achieve its biologically determined ends or goals (2007, p. 121). If an animal is incapable of acting other than on the basis of biologically determined ends, then it can be said to be acting without reason. And so, we can observe animals for behaviours that display instrumental rationality as they will be the ones that demonstrate the ability to learn. Behavioural markers for learning new ways to achieve goals show that an agent is able to generate new goals and infer beliefs, which means that they can reliably be said to have reasons for their actions

(Okrent 2007, p. 122). This view makes sense of the differences in behaviours that can be observed among members of the same species, as each individual's actions will be determined by their own particular beliefs. If an individual believes that a certain action will help them to achieve their particular goal, then it will modify its behaviour accordingly. These individual beliefs count as reasons that motivate actions, and they allow for the ability to act intentionally.

Another related approach to the explanation of animal behaviours as intentional is to describe them as *goal-directed*. Often, animal behaviours are described as goal-oriented, in that they are a result of evolution, whereby if an action is performed within a suitable environment, then the animal will achieve its goal. Goal-oriented behaviours are not the result of mental representations possessed by the animal, but are the result of generations of selection that bestow survival and reproductive benefits. These sorts of actions and behaviours are not intentional. However, if an animal acts as a result of mental representations it has of its own goals and how to achieve them, referring to animals as goal-directed is a more accurate way to account for these behaviours, and this means that such actions are intentional. Eric Saidel (2009) argues for a view of animal agency as goal-directed behaviour, and this is particularly useful for making the distinction between animals (including humans) as intentional agents and other objects, such as plants or inorganic artefacts. This distinction may seem like common sense, but it will become more important in subsequent chapters of this book as it establishes the basis for moral categories, such as the difference between having direct moral obligations towards animals, and indirect moral obligations towards objects such as plants or ecosystems. To the extent that Saidel's arguments support the claim that animals are intentional agents, they also support my claim that we owe animals direct moral obligations as autonomous, acting agents (see Chap. 4).

Saidel's main claim is that "behavior that is appropriately explained in terms of mental states such as beliefs and desires is behavior directed at a goal relative to which the agent is able to *learn*; and since human behavior meets this criterion, I argue, we should expect, on evolutionary grounds, that some animal behavior meets this criterion as well" (2009, p. 35). As such, he adopts a realist position regarding belief-desire explanations, such that any behaviour that is accurately explained as a result of assuming beliefs and desires is considered to genuinely possess them, and that they cause the behaviour being examined. He wants to argue that some animal behaviours are caused by such mental states, and this is what establishes the grounds for attributing intentionality to animals.

Saidel contends that both beliefs and desires are forms of representations or internal mental states of both the world as it is, and the way the animal wants it to be. While remaining agnostic as to the "true" nature of these representations (as we have previously examined when questioning whether or not animals possess concepts), he simply claims that animals have some kind of mental representation of their goals and what they need to do to achieve them. These representations cause the animal to act in accordance with their desires. Although Saidel does not explicitly call this agency, it seems to count towards an explanation of what is needed to be an agent at its most basic level, which is the ability to direct one's own behaviour in accordance with one's goals, beliefs, desires, and preferences. There must be some mental content, in these forms, even minimally, that causes one to act at all. This is what allows for the distinction between agents and other objects, as agents act as a result of distinct mental representations, whereas plants "act" as a result of goal-oriented causes. Indeed, Saidel describes how some plants move in such a way as to follow the sun as a result of chemical reactions between the light from the sun and chemicals in the plant. This behaviour is goal-oriented, as it is not based on mental representations of any kind, but is the result of an evolutionary mechanism that helps the plant achieve a particular goal. The goal itself plays no role in the movement of the plants, but is oriented by evolution to achieve a particular goal. Such behaviour can be found in some animals as well, such as stereotypical behaviour that is beneficial from an evolutionary perspective, and which the animal performs without needing any mental representation of its goal (Saidel 2009, p. 38).

Goal-directed behaviour is contrasted with goal-oriented behaviour as the first is based on a representation of a particular goal, and the animal acts in such a way as to achieve that goal. Examples of this provided by Saidel include rats navigating a maze or chimpanzees cracking nuts on rocks using sticks, both of which demonstrate the ability to "abandon one behaviour and adopt another while still retaining the goal that the previous behaviour was aimed at achieving, and toward which the new behaviour is now directed" (2009, p. 39). Goal-directed behaviour thus requires a kind of learning that only some animals are capable of. They have the ability to learn specific ways to achieve their goals by forming new associations with their goals. For Saidel, the main point is that animals would not be able to act in a goal-directed fashion unless they possessed mental representations of both the means to achieve their ends, and a representation of those ends. Attributing beliefs and desires to these animals is simply the best way to explain their behaviours. In this way, Saidel is in agreement with both Dennett and de Waal, as he posits that the methodology of adopting the intentional stance is both useful and accurate in explaining the behaviour of animals. He differs from Dennett, however, in his distinction between goal-oriented and goal-directed behaviours and, in doing so, reinforces the distinction between animals and other objects that relates to intentionality. For Dennett, the intentional stance can be applied to both animals and other objects, such as machines. This is problematic as it disallows for the idea that there is something different, in ontologically and morally relevant ways, between animals and other objects. Why, for example, should we care more about the intentionality of a dog than an air conditioner? Saidel provides us with one such way as he focuses on the element of learning to distinguish goal-directed behaviour from goal-oriented behaviour, the former being a feature exclusive to those who possess mental representations, namely, animals (human and non-human). This, as I will argue, is what makes intentional agents, such as animals, proper recipients of direct moral consideration, while objects like air conditioners and other non-mental objects are not.

To resist ascribing intentionality to animals is problematic at best and simply mistaken at worst. One reason why someone might be reluctant to do so is based on a fear of anthropomorphism. This view holds that when we ascribe "human" traits or characteristics to animals we are generally not justified in doing so. It may indeed be the case that anthropomorphizing can lead to improper or inaccurate ascriptions or claims about the explanations of animal behaviours, and this can in itself be harmful to animals. It could also be argued that we ought not to ascribe complex cognitive abilities to animals if we are able to explain their behaviours in non-mentalistic terms, similar to the psychological behaviourism approach to studying minds. There are further concerns that relate to the ascription of beliefs to animals, in that we could be making incorrect belief ascriptions as a result of anthropomorphizing animal behaviours. However, the fear of anthropomorphism can prevent us from taking animal minds as legitimate objects of study, and the harms that result are greater than the potential mistakes we may make when ascribing mental and cognitive abilities to animals. Indeed, Frans de Waal (2006) responds to this fear by arguing that to dismiss the attribution of cognitive states to animals *a priori* can be called "anthropodenial". It is a mistake, according to de Waal, to reject the notion that humans and animals share characteristics and possess similar behaviours. He says that "while it is true that animals are not humans, it is equally true that humans are animals. Resistance to this simple yet undeniable truth is what underlies the resistance to anthropomorphism." (2006, p. 65) Anthropodenial, then, can be seen as a deeper resistance to accepting the more basic fact that we are all animals and that, by virtue of this fact, we share common traits and characteristics with other species. For some, accepting this truth poses a threat to human superiority over other animals, and challenges the ways in which this superiority is reflected in our relationships with them. If we can overcome this anthropodenial, then we can see the usefulness of explaining and predicting animal behaviour by ascribing cognitive terms to the study of animal minds. To use such language, just as Dennett argues, is valuable and useful for the scientific study of animals. De Waal explains the importance of using anthropomorphic language in a critical way as a tool for getting at the truth:

> Obviously, if anthropomorphism is defined as the misattribution of human qualities to animals, no one wishes to be associated with it. But much of the time, a broader definition is employed, namely the description of animal behaviour in human, hence intentionalistic, terms. Even though no anthropomorphism proponent would propose to apply such language uncritically, even the staunchest opponents of anthropomorphism do not deny its value as an heuristic tool. It is this use of anthropomorphism as a means to get at the truth, rather than as an end in itself, that distinguishes its use in science from that by the layperson. The ultimate goal of the

anthropomorphizing scientist is emphatically not the most satisfactory projection of human feelings onto the animal, but testable ideas and replicable observations. (2006, p. 63)

When we apply intentional terms to animal behaviours, which we would normally apply to human behaviours, we are not making any claims that what goes on in an animal mind and what goes on in a human mind is exactly the same thing. Most would agree that we cannot with any certainty know what it is like to be in an animal's mind, or to think like an animal, just as we cannot do so with another human being. And we are certainly tempted, as common usage indicates, to over-ascribe human traits to animals, such as when we call an old dog wise, or a cat reserved. De Waal's point, however, is that in science anthropomorphism can be used critically and with the goal of creating claims that are testable. By placing these restrictions and parameters on the use of anthropomorphism we can avoid the pitfalls of misattribution. This also addresses concerns about incorrectly ascribing beliefs to animals, as it helps to keep ascriptions made by laypersons and those made by scientists distinct, since in each case a different meaning of belief is being used. But it is both premature and inaccurate to dismiss the possibility altogether that what goes on in the minds of animals is not similar to what goes on in the minds of humans. We can, in many cases, successfully predict and explain animal behaviour using intentional language in a critical way, as it is the most logical method to use and apply to the study of animal minds. Dennett and de Waal agree on this methodology, as do most cognitive psychologists and ethologists, which shows that anthropodenial is both unjustified and inaccurate.

Moral Agency

As the study of animal ethics continues to grow, new questions and topics arise within the field. One of these areas of study addresses whether or not animals can act morally. If animals are acting agents that are motivated by reasons, can those reasons ever be moral? On the one hand, it is overwhelmingly accepted that animals cannot be morally responsible for their actions, and we tend to consider them as moral patients, or simply those to whom we owe moral consideration or obligations, but who are not capable of acting morally towards others. On the other hand, more recent research has discovered that some animals seem to act in ways that are most appropriately described as moral. As such, we are presented with new questions to consider. Can any animal action be said to be truly moral in nature? If it can, does it change their moral status? If we think there are only two categories—moral patients who themselves cannot act morally; and moral agents, or those who act for moral reasons and can thus be held morally responsible for their actions—where do animals fit in?

Moral agency is generally understood as the ability to act morally, based on moral reasons, which makes the agent responsible for their actions. This requires metacognitive abilities, which means that an agent is able to reflect on or consider their reasons for acting. In other words, metacognition is the ability to know what we know, or be aware of what we know. Some studies have attempted to find this in animals, although it is difficult to devise experiments for this purpose. Based on these studies, it seems that some primates, and perhaps dolphins, are able to show this ability consistently (Shettleworth and Sutton 2006). Even if animals possess beliefs, desires, and concepts, it is generally agreed that they are unable to reflect on them or rationally evaluate them in ways that grant them moral agency. Instead, animals are generally viewed as moral patients, whereby they are treated as morally considerable by those who are moral agents. This means that for most, humans are the only creatures who possess moral agency, and who can act for moral reasons. This is important, as it relates to agency more generally in the sense that we recognize moral agents as those who possess rights and who are autonomous, thus granting them special moral status and respect as persons. In this chapter I am arguing that animals are acting agents, in ways that are both minimal and rich, depending on the complexity of beliefs and concepts possessed by individual animals. The ability to act freely, in accordance with one's beliefs and desires, and to achieve certain goals, is what grounds the importance of autonomy in terms of respecting that freedom to act. However, if some animals are able to act based on moral reasons, it would mean that some animals are agents in a richer sense still, thus strengthening the argument that some animals are acting, autonomous agents. And so, it is important to review some of the current arguments in favour of the moral agency of animals, to which I turn now.

One view on the moral agency of animals is that morality is a trait shared by humans and animals by virtue of the evolutionary continuity among species. De Waal (2006) argues that empathy and sympathy, for example, provide an evolutionary advantage and survival value to those who possess them, and that the difference between animals and humans in their ability to demonstrate such traits is a result of the effects of language and culture, which allow for humans to simply have more expressions of them than other animals (24). He believes that the tendency to overlook the emotional capacities of animals in science and cognitive studies more generally is a result of the traditional focus on the individual rather than inter-individual or social capacities, which form the basis of morality itself. Indeed, he argues that the best sorts of evidence of intelligence or higher cognitive capacities in animals comes from the social domain, as it requires the ability to identify, evaluate, and respond to the emotional states of others in order to survive within groups (de Waal 2006, p. 27). After reviewing examples of primate empathy, de Waal concludes that perhaps only elephants and dolphins, along with primates, are capable of true "helping responses", although this does not entail that other animals do not possess empathy. In fact, it would seem more plausible that other social animals who have a more complex sense of self-awareness would also possess such traits, as they have a greater understanding of the difference between self and other such that they can identify when another animal needs help and address it (such as through consolation, for example) (de Waal 2006, pp. 33–36). De Waal also argues that a more egocentric (than humans) sense of reciprocity and fairness can be seen in animals, and believes that underlying the ability to be moral is having a sense of self, and that morality then, is a part of human nature and something that is continuous across species (2006, p. 49). He believes that it is a mistake to think that as natural selection is a seemingly cruel process, it can only produce cruel creatures. Instead, he argues that,

> nature's pressure cooker does not work that way. It favors organisms that survive and reproduce, pure and simple. How they accomplish that is left

open. Any organism that can do better by becoming either more or less aggressive than the rest, more or less cooperative, or more or less caring, will spread its genes. (de Waal 2006, p. 58)

For de Waal, full moral agency is possessed by humans and this is demonstrated by their ability to create moral theories and principles that are universally applicable. Other animals do not possess this ability, and so are not full moral agents in terms of having moral systems and moral responsibility for their actions. However, in his view, moral agency is a matter of degree, as the emotional responses all animals have towards each other form the basis of moral behaviours and social cooperation. Moral feelings and behaviours are continuous across animal species, and so de Waal supports an evolutionary theory of ethics. This view supports the idea that animals are agents and self-aware to varying degrees, as the emotions he cites as minimally moral require some awareness of the difference between self and other, along with beliefs and concepts that provide the grounds for acting. De Waal's view has been referred to as one that views animals as proto-moral, in the sense that animals possess the rudiments of morality while not being fully moral agents. Only in humans, from this viewpoint, do we find moral agents who are capable of acting on the basis of reasons. And so, even though de Waal provides an account of moral agency as existing on a gradient, he does not go so far as to call animals themselves moral in the same way that humans are.

Evelyn B. Pluhar (2013) similarly argues that the roots of morality, such as altruism and empathy, can be found in animals, and that it is a serious mistake to claim that morality is the "exclusive province of humans" (197). She believes that in maintaining the idea that only humans are moral agents, it not only puts humans in a category separate from other animals, but it also places humans above other animals, thereby also asserting that humans are the only morally considerable beings on the planet. By arguing that moral agency exists on an evolutionary continuum, she hopes to challenge the anthropocentric view that only humans count, morally. Pluhar argues that it is plausible to claim that animals are capable of altruism and empathy, based on the weight of evidence provided by biology, psychology, ethology, and anecdotal accounts (2013, p. 201). She supports the first claim, that animals are altruistic, with the notion that such a feature has evolutionary benefits as it increases reproductive success and survival. This is because the abilities to nurture, bond, cooperate, and adapt provide the basis of stability for humans and animals living in groups, in the form of caring relationships. Altruistic behaviours occur between family members, but it has also been noted that social animals display the same behaviours toward other individuals that are not related to them. This can be explained through reciprocity, where an animal can receive benefits from showing altruistic behaviours towards another unrelated animal, in terms of things like food sharing. Pluhar provides many examples of animals assisting other animals across species, and sometimes assisting others, even at the risk of putting themselves in danger. Although this may seem to run counter to idea that altruistic acts are driven by the urge to survive, and so only occur due to kinship or reciprocity, it is possible to argue that the actual ability to recognize and respond to the needs of others predisposes some individuals to care about strangers they cannot derive a benefit from (Pluhar 2013, p. 207). For Pluhar, "Empathy, and emotions in general, are keystones of moral behavior, including self-sacrificial altruism. Although, as we shall see, reasoning is also required for full moral agency, it is not the prime factor." (2013, p. 208) In making a distinction between degrees of moral agency, Pluhar is acknowledging that only a minimal level of agency is required for moral action. Full moral agency requires the kind of rational reflection that most normal, adult humans possess, but minimal moral agency only requires the ability to act as a result of empathy, as it is the basis for all other levels of moral agency.

Another important aspect of Pluhar's argument is that for anyone, human or animal, to have empathy or sympathy, a sense of self is required. Being able to recognize someone as distinct from oneself is what enables sympathy or empathy to exist. And so, Pluhar examines how we might know that a human or animal has a sense of self. She considers mirror self-recognition tests as one form of evidence for self-awareness, and there are animals that can pass this test, but she does not consider that failing the test shows a lack of self-awareness. This is due to the kinds of challenges that result from different species possessing different traits that might prevent them from responding to the test in expected ways. Looking at research on young human children however, it is possible to see that even without the ability for full self-reflection, control over one's actions in a goal-directed manner can occur in children as young as two months. She argues that many non-human animals also develop such abilities at a young age as part of what is necessary for survival, and refers to de Waal's (2009) view that empathy is multilayered, and progresses from simple emotional contagion to the targeted helping of others, which requires a sense of self that allows one to grasp others' points of view. Further to this, Pluhar notes that members of social species also need to be able to identify and assess the intentions of others to know how to best respond to them (2013, p. 219). An example of this is playing behaviour, as it requires perspective taking and the assessment of another's intentions in order to participate. She says that, along with humans, there is evidence that mammals and birds also engage in playing behaviours (2013, p. 221). When members of various social species recognize unfair behaviour they may punish those who violate accepted rules, indicating that they have a sense of a correct social order. All these examples and arguments lead Pluhar to conclude that,

> We have seen that nonhuman animals and even very young humans are agents who possess the basis for moral behavior: empathy and fairness. This accounts for the numerous instances of altruistic behavior observed in many species besides our own. We might call these nonhumans and small children incipient moral agents. Nonetheless, fully blown moral agency is not present in the very young, or, as far as we know, in nonhumans of any age. (2013, p. 221)

Non-human animals and small children are agents insofar as they have a sense of self, and can act on the basis of empathy, sympathy, and fairness, which results from an understanding and assessment of the actions and intentions of others. In Pluhar's account, agency is on a continuum from a minimal level that enables individuals to act intentionally, to fully reflective agents that not only act intentionally, but who also have moral responsibilities and duties towards others. She believes that although animals are acting agents, and that this entitles them to rights of freedom and well-being, they are unable to recognize the universalizability of these rights in order to limit their own actions towards others in the same ways that humans do (Pluhar 2013, pp. 222–223). This way of arguing that animals are minimally moral, and therefore not responsible for their actions, can be seen as dissatisfactory by some, who believe that moral agency and responsibility are inseparable. This poses a problem as, if we understand animals to be moral agents, however minimally, then they must be responsible for their own actions on at least some level. This concern provides the basis for another view on animals and moral agency, which I will now examine.

A more detailed account of animals being able to act morally is provided by Mark Rowlands (2011, 2012), who argues that although animals are not moral agents in the sense of being able to reflect rationally on their reasons for acting, they are moral subjects who act on the basis of moral emotions. For Rowlands, acting on the basis of moral emotions is sufficient for acting morally, and animals are able to act as a result of moral concerns, which amount to emotions that have an identifiable moral content. He does not deny that humans are able to act on the basis of reasons that are unavailable to animals, since humans are able to reflect on and rationally evaluate their moral motivations, and they are able to create abstract principles that allow them to judge their own actions and to communicate these principles to others (2012, p. 37). However, he argues that animals are moral subjects as they can be motivated to act by moral considerations, and these considerations take the form of morally laden emotions such as sympathy, compassion, tolerance, patience, indifference, anger, malice, and spite. Morally laden emotions involve a moral evaluation and judgment, and Rowlands argues that these emotions motivate animals to act, thereby providing reasons for those actions (2012, pp. 34–35). As these can be considered reasons for acting and not merely causes for acting, he believes they provide the element of normativity needed to properly call some animals moral subjects.

To make his argument, Rowlands argues that emotion, in the sense that is relevant to moral subjectivity, is identifiable with intentional states that have both descriptive and prescriptive content. As such, he spends time defending the claim that animals possess concepts and can act intentionally, as I have outlined earlier in this chapter. However, further to this, he argues that emotions involve both factual and evaluative judgments, and that, "Emotions, if they are legitimate, track true evaluative propositions, but they do not require that the subject of an emotion entertain, or even be capable of entertaining, such a proposition." (Rowlands 2012, p. 67) In this way, an animal can possess a morally laden emotion that is intentional and content-involving without needing to possess the ability to consciously and rationally reflect on or evaluate it. This means that animals can properly be ascribed mental content and concepts, and that they act intentionally on the basis of such content even if they are unable to evaluate it. For an animal to be a minimal moral subject it requires the ability to have beliefs and emotions. Rowlands says that a minimal moral subject can be described in the following way:

> X is a *moral subject* if X possesses (1) a sensitivity to the good- or bad-making features of situations, where (2) this sensitivity can be normatively assessed, and (3) is grounded in the operations of a reliable mechanism (a "moral module"). (2012, p. 230)

An animal, as a moral subject, experiences emotions based on the situation they are in, and these emotions are intentionally directed towards the beliefs involved in having those emotions. For example, upon seeing another animal's suffering, a dog might feel sympathy for it, and that emotion counts as a reason for the dog's resulting action towards the other animal. This does not make an animal a moral agent, as they are unable to evaluate their actions and the possible consequences of them in the same ways that humans can. It does mean however, that the ability to act morally can be understood as existing along a continuum from minimally moral actions to fully moral actions, which is dependent on the complexity of the mental capacities for belief and concept formation and possession that an individual possesses. Putting this in the context of what I am arguing for within this chapter, a minimal agent is able to act intentionally on the basis of beliefs and concepts without needing to be able to rationally evaluate them in the same way a complex and fully rational agent can. The ability to act intentionally, in general and morally, is then a matter of degree rather than of kind.

Conclusion

In this chapter, I have argued that some animals are acting, intentional agents by virtue of their ability to possess beliefs and concepts, and their capacity for reason. Although these arguments can still be contested, there is a broad consensus that, despite the difficulties in studying the exact nature of how animals think and perceive the world, they ought to be considered creatures with minds and intentions of their own. Agency is what separates animals from other objects, such as plants, and is what provides the grounds for moral consideration, as they are creatures that can act on the basis of reasons and free choice. The specific capacities required for agency, such as rationality and intentionality, exist in varying degrees among individual animals, both across and within species, and this is supported through evidence from multiple research sources in the sciences and social sciences. Recent views of animals as moral agents and moral subjects demonstrate that animal agency is a reasonable and acceptable assumption that allows for new considerations to be made that challenge our notions of the complexities of animal thinking. In the next chapter I argue that some animals are also self-aware in varying degrees, which provides the grounds for arguing that some animals can also be considered autonomous, and thus are owed direct moral obligations.

References

Allen, C. (1999). Animal concepts revisited: The use of self-monitoring as an empirical approach. *Erkenntnis, 51*, 33–40.

Allen, C. (2013). The geometry of partial understanding. *American Philosophical Quarterly, 50*(3), 249–262.

Allen, C., & Bekoff, M. (2007). Animals minds, cognitive ethology, and ethics. *The Journal of Ethics, 11*, 299–317.

Andrews, K. (2012). Animal cognition. In E. N. Zalta (Ed.), *The Stanford encyclopedia of philosophy* (Winter ed.). Retrieved from http://plato.stanford.edu/archives/win2012/entries/cognition-animal

Andrews, K. (2015). *The animal mind: An introduction to the philosophy of animal cognition*. New York: Routledge.

Bekoff, M. (2006a). Animal emotions and animal sentience and why they matter: Blending 'science sense' with common sense, compassion and heart. In J. Turner & J. D'Silva (Eds.), *Animals, ethics and trade: The challenge of animal sentience* (pp. 27–40). London: Earthscan.

Dennett, D. C. (1995). Do animals have beliefs? In H. L. Roitblat & J.-A. Meyer (Eds.), *Comparative approaches to cognitive science.* (pp. 111–118). Cambridge: The MIT Press.

Dennett, D. C. (2012). Intentional systems theory, pp. 1–22. Tufts University. Retrieved October 10, 2013, from http://ase.tufts.edu/cogstud/dennett/papers/intentionalsystems.pdf

de Waal, F. (2006). *Primates and philosophers: How morality evolved.* Princeton: Princeton University Press.

de Waal, F. (2009). *The age of empathy: Nature's lessons for a kinder society.* Toronto: McClelland & Stewart Ltd.

Dretske, F. I. (2006). Minimal rationality. In S. Hurley & M. Nudds (Eds.), *Rational animals?* (pp. 107–115). Toronto: Oxford University Press.

Glock, H.-J. (2013). Mental capacities and animal ethics. In K. Petrus & M. Wild (Eds.), *Animal minds & animal ethics: Connecting two separate fields* (pp. 113–146). Bielefeld: transcript Verlag.

O'Brien, L. (2015). *Philosophy of action.* Basingstoke: Palgrave Macmillan.

Okrent, M. (2007). *Rational animals: The teleological roots of intentionality.* Athens: Ohio University Press.

Pluhar, E. B. (2013). The nonhuman roots of human morality. In K. Petrus & M. Wild (Eds.), *Animal minds & animal ethics: Connecting two separate fields* (pp. 197–227). Bielefeld: transcript Verlag.

Rowlands, M. (2011). Animals that act for moral reasons. In T. L. Beauchamp & R. G. Frey (Eds.), *The Oxford handbook of animal ethics* (pp. 1–19). New York: Oxford University Press.

Rowlands, M. (2012). *Can animals be moral?* Toronto: Oxford University Press.

Saidel, E. (2009). Attributing mental representations to animals. In R. W. Lurz (Ed.), *The philosophy of animal minds* (pp. 35–51). New York: Cambridge University Press.

Shettleworth, S. J., & Sutton, J. E. (2006). Do animals know what they know? In S. Hurley & M. Nudds (Eds.), *Rational animals* (pp. 235–246). Toronto: Oxford University Press.

3

Self-Awareness and Selfhood in Animals

Introduction

Self-awareness is an important feature of agency, as it allows one to be aware of one's own beliefs, desires, and preferences, even if only in a minimal sense. Perhaps most importantly, self-awareness allows one to have preferences, which can determine one's choices among various options for acting. This further relates to autonomy, as we value the freedom to make our own choices, good or bad, as a result of what we value. I argue in Chap. 4 that when we restrict the ability to make free choices, we restrict autonomy. And so, the importance of asking whether or not animals are self-aware is crucial to the establishment of animal autonomy. I argue that there are good reasons for accepting the view that many animals are, in fact, self-aware, based on both empirical research and on the basis of arguments that self-awareness is a feature of conscious creatures who act intentionally. In particular, I argue that self-awareness exists in varying degrees, from a minimal sense to a much more complex, or rich sense, both across and within species. My goal is not to draw a strict line between those who possess self-awareness and those who do not, but rather to establish that it is justifiable to claim that many animal species are self-aware in ways that make them morally considerable.

Self-Consciousness and Self-Awareness

Self-awareness, then, is an important feature of consciousness by virtue of its moral significance. It is however, also considered to be the "hard problem" within the field of consciousness studies generally. Broadly construed, "self-awareness means to be aware of one's own feelings or emotions and to be conscious of pain, but self-awareness also includes awareness of one's body (e.g. allowing recognition of oneself in a mirror), one's state of mind, one's self in a social context, and numerous other, ill-defined attributes that we would assign ourselves." (Griffin 2001, p. 14). This is referred to as the hard problem because, according to Marion Stamp Dawkins (2012): "The distinction between the easy and hard problems of consciousness is the distinction between giving an explanation for complex behaviour or changing brain states, on the one hand, and giving an explanation for why that behaviour or those changing brain states are accompanied by conscious experiences, on the other." (46). Indeed, it is important to note that nobody has so far provided an account of self-consciousness or self-awareness that has firmly or decidedly solved the hard problem. What we can do is examine some of the various attempts to define and understand self-awareness as something that is given in our own conscious experiences. So, while these definitions admit to the problematic ambiguity of the concept of self-awareness, they also, and more importantly, indicate that there are degrees to such an awareness of oneself, from a basic sense of one's own body and one's feelings, to a more complex awareness of oneself and others that is required for social interactions. As humans, we often refer to someone who is self-aware as a person who has reflected on the kind of person they want to be, and ways in which they can improve themselves. But there is a more basic way in which we are aware of ourselves in a bodily sense, in terms of things like an awareness that our feet are hurting or that we feel hunger. As we recognize these feelings and sensations as belonging to us, they count as forms of self-awareness, even if in a more minimal sense than the person who aims towards self-improvement.

3 Self-Awareness and Selfhood in Animals

In the attempt to clarify the concept of self-awareness, I am arguing that there are two main levels of self-awareness, which are minimal and rich. This is despite the fact that some people define self-awareness only at higher-order levels, where "our thoughts and experiences become available to us for introspection: we can think about what we think, and know what we know." (Rogers 1997, p. 15). This view of self-awareness is what allows for a personal identity, or an I-ness, where one's self can become an object of examination and reflection. Cheney and Seyfarth (2007) explain that "an explicit sense of self emerges in children at roughly the same age as the ability to attribute knowledge and beliefs to others" (203). It is this explicit sense of self that is considered exclusive to humans and some other animals, including primates, elephants, and dolphins, in part due to their ability to successfully pass mirror self-recognition tests that indicate an advanced understanding of the difference between self and other. This seems problematic, however, if we consider that different species might not pass self-recognition tests due to differences between "primary sensory modalities of recognition" (Bekoff and Sherman 2004, p. 178). In other words, depending on the individual and species, an animal may not respond to mirror self-recognition tests not due to a lack of self-recognition or self-awareness, but because of the difficulties in devising such tests to suit the variations in the senses that they possess and how these affect their ability to perceive themselves and their own reflections. Furthermore, it can be argued that minimal levels of self-awareness can exist without an explicit sense of personal identity, and these degrees of selfhood can be explained, in part, as a result of biological theories or observations that have been made in cognitive ethology. For example, Bekoff and Sherman (2004) argue that:

> The position of an individual on the self-cognizance continuum is determined, ultimately, by natural selection, based on the degree to which members of its species or group (e.g. males or females) repeat competitive or cooperative interactions with the same conspecifics over their lifetimes and benefit from changing their responses in light of outcomes of those previous interactions. (177)

They stress the point that self-cognizance is a matter of degree, both across species and among individuals, rather than a matter of kind. Bekoff and Sherman (2004) have provided a useful schema for differentiating between self-referencing, self-awareness, and self-consciousness, as degrees of self-cognizance. Self-referencing refers to the ability to discriminate between another individual and themselves, based on odour or appearance for example, to accept or reject that individual as belonging to the same phenotype. This can occur consciously or non-consciously. Self-awareness is also described as perceptual consciousness, body-ness, or mine-ness. This is the cognitive ability to discriminate between one's own body and those of others, or between territory or possessions as mine or as belonging to another individual. Creatures that are self-aware may or may not be conscious, according to Bekoff and Sherman. Finally, self-consciousness is the broadest category, which includes: reflective consciousness: sense of self: self-reflection: I-ness: having sympathy or empathy: and a theory of mind. All individuals in this category are conscious, and Bekoff and Sherman speculate that self-consciousness evolves from benefits gained when being able to revise one's own behaviours as responses to other members of one's own social group. It leads to more finely tuned behaviours as it requires knowledge of the differences between oneself and others, and memories involving previous social interactions (Bekoff and Sherman 2004, p. 177). Importantly, the main emphasis of their research establishes that selfhood is found at more than just the richest level that we associate with humans, and that it exists in more minimal levels in other animal species.

Self-awareness, in its less complex levels, has been described as a sense of mine-ness, or phenomenal self-awareness. This level of self-awareness also means that there is "something it is like" to be that particular animal. One view that captures this level of self-awareness is described by Marc Bekoff (2003) as mine-ness or as a sense of body-ness. This level of self-awareness is more complex than simple perceptions of stimuli in the external world, which is also referred to as sentience. Bekoff explains body-ness or mine-ness in the following way: "Thus, for example, some experimental treatment, object, or other individual might cause pain, and the receiving individual says something like: 'Something is happening to this body, and I had better do something about it.' There is no need to associate *this* body with *my* body or 'me' (or 'I')." (2003, p. 232) Further to this, he describes how his dog, Jethro, obviously knew that he was not his dog friend, Zeke. He argues that most animals are able to identify objects as their own (i.e., "this is my toy, or my mate", etc.), and that this knowledge is what allows animals to function in their own "worlds". Bekoff says:

He (Jethro) and other animals have a sense of possession or a sense of mine-ness, or body-ness, if you will. So, in this way they have a sense of self… Jethro could communicate a wide variety of messages, socially interact in numerous and varied contexts, and enjoy life as a dog. So, too, can chimpanzees, rhesus monkeys, wolves, bears, crows, sweat bees, ants, and many others animals…He (Jethro) also showed social self-awareness in that he was aware of his various and different relationships with others. Whether or not he had an introspective self and a theory of his and others' minds remains unknown. It surely would be premature to conclude that he did not. (2003, p. 233)

From this point of view, selfhood in its minimal sense refers to an awareness of oneself and others, which then allows an individual to interact with others in social relationships. This sense of mine-ness does not require a full or rich sense of personal identity, or even a theory of mind, but it does require a level of consciousness whereby an animal is simply aware of its own body, which allows that animal to respond to objects and other animals in appropriate ways. For me to acknowledge this pain as belonging to me, there must be a "me" there, or a subject that experiences this pain as my own. This sense of self is immediate, and basic to all conscious creatures, including most animals. If there was no sense of self, even minimally for an individual, there would be nothing to which the experience belonged, or no one to experience the pain.

Dan Zahavi (2005) also argues in favour of less complex levels of selfhood saying: "Contrary to what some of the self-skeptics are claiming, one does not need to conceive of the self as something standing apart from or above experiences, nor does one need to conceive of the relation between self and experience as an external relation of ownership. It is also possible to identify this pre-reflective sense of mine-ness with a minimal, or core, sense of self." (2005, p. 125) This sense of mine-ness can also be described as phenomenal consciousness, which is simply the feeling that accompanies self-awareness. Minimal self-awareness, or a core sense of self, can exist without a complex sense of self-identity, or the ability to take oneself as an object of reflection. This level of mine-ness can also be described as phenomenal consciousness, which refers to "the qualitative, subjective, experiential, or phenomenological aspects of conscious experience, sometimes identified with qualia" (Allen 2013). Because this form of self-awareness is so difficult to describe in words, it can be easily questioned or doubted as existing at all. This relates to the problem of knowing other minds, as the very nature of our own thoughts and feelings are private and subjective. How can we know for certain that others experience consciousness in the same ways that we do? This problem is difficult enough when we consider the minds of other humans, but it is compounded when we attempt make claims about the contents of animal minds.

Those who are extremely sceptical take issue with the epistemological issues raised by the topic of knowing other minds. For them, the idea of access to other minds across species would be laughable. For, as Nagel (1979) argues, although there is surely something it is like to be a bat, we can never know, through science, observation, or description, what it is *actually* like to be a bat. And certainly, I do not know what it is like to have wings and fly, but neither do I know what it is like to be blind, or to be a man, for that matter. The significant point in determining if animals have a sense of self or self-awareness is whether or not they are capable of having experiences of what it is like to be them, rather than determining what it is *actually* like to be them. Even with verbal descriptions, we cannot know exactly what it is like to have the experiences that other humans have. But this by no means prevents us from believing that other humans are self-aware or that they are subject experiences and thoughts like we are.

If animals are phenomenally conscious, then they have a self, at least in a form less complex than found in humans. This is a result of the nature of experience and perception, which requires a subject, as a property of consciousness. As Zahavi (2005) describes, "there is a minimal sense of self present whenever there is self-awareness. Self-awareness is there not only when I realize that I am perceiving a candle, but whenever I am acquainted with an experience in its first-personal mode of givenness, that is, whenever there is something it is like for me to have the experience. In other words, pre-reflective self-awareness and a minimal sense of self are integral parts of our experiential life." (146) Zahavi further writes in a footnote to this passage that:

> If this is true, it has some rather obvious consequences for the attribution of both self and self-consciousness to animals. It is also obvious, of course, that there are higher and more complex forms of self-consciousness that most, if not all, nonhuman animals lack. As for the question of where to draw the line, i.e., whether it also makes sense to ascribe a sense of self to

lower organisms such as birds, amphibians, fish, beetles, worms, etc., this is a question that I will leave for others to decide. All I will say is that if a certain organism is in possession of phenomenal consciousness, then it must also be in possession of both a primitive form of self-consciousness and a core self. (2005, pp. 235–236)

The core self is a useful term to denote the most minimal form of selfhood, which has also been described in this chapter as mine-ness, body-ness, and as phenomenal consciousness. It is indeed difficult, as Zahavi notes, to draw the line between those species and individuals that possess a minimal sense of self, and those that do not. Presumably, there is a certain point where it is inappropriate and inaccurate to ascribe a sense of self to individuals and species. However, if a creature possesses any mental capacities that suggest the possible possession of self-awareness, then it is safer and more prudent to err on the side of caution and treat it as self-aware rather than not. So, even if an animal possesses a sense of mine-ness or body-ness, but not a rich sense of personal identity, nor a fully reflective form of self-consciousness that most humans possess, it is considered to be indicative of selfhood nonetheless. Selfhood is not the kind of mental characteristic that either exists in its richest form or not at all, but rather it exists in degrees across species and among conscious individuals, and it can be indicated by the existence of a variety of mental capacities and capabilities, some of which are examined later in this chapter.

A relevant argument that supports the existence of self-awareness in animals is made by DeGrazia (2009), who claims that self-awareness is required for intentional behavior, based on the belief-desire model of intentional action. He claims that "Much behavior among sentient animals suggests desires. Much of this same behavior, I submit, is best understood as reflecting beliefs that, together with the relevant desires, produce intentional action." (2009, p. 204) DeGrazia admits, as do Saidel and Dennett, that beliefs and desires are difficult to define, but that despite these problems we can generalize that animals do have mental representations based on perceptions that provide content, affording the grounds or reasons for their actions. Desires and intentional actions require a sense of oneself as persisting through time and, even if only rudimentary, this requires self-awareness and the ability to desire the intended goal, create a plan to achieve it, and form a representation of completing the plan.

DeGrazia claims that, "If this is correct, then a common-sense appreciation of the ordinary behaviors of many animals suggests a kind of self-awareness—namely, bodily self-awareness, here with an emphasis on the agency aspect." (2009, p. 205) After citing various studies of animals using tools and solving problems, DeGrazia concludes that such evidence supports the claim that intentional action is only possible if these animals have a sense of themselves persisting in time long enough to achieve their goals, a sense of their own bodies as distinct from the rest of their environment, and of their bodies as subjects of their own direct control. In this way, DeGrazia provides an important connection between beliefs, desires, and preferences and the self-awareness needed to possess such capabilities in order to be considered an intentional agent. Without self-awareness, animals could not act in goal-directed ways, or with intentionality.

The idea that language is required for beliefs and concepts is related to a similar problem in the study of self-awareness, as some argue that self-consciousness is the ability to know that one is experiencing internal events. To be able to take one's own experiences as the objects of reflection requires, for some, higher-order consciousness, as this allows for the ability to do such things as think about one's past or future, or engage in self-talk, self-evaluation, and so on. Alain Morin (2012) describes the ability to use language to self-regulate as something only humans can do, as they can use inner speech to alter their own behaviours, change their own moods, or select a response from various options, for example. Humans are also subject to problems that result from excessive self-focus, like social anxiety, depression, and even suicide, whereas these problems do not seem to affect animals, at least to the same extent. And so, Morin suggests that self-awareness is constituted by a variety of mental capacities, and that while both animals and humans share many of them, humans have a more complex level of self-awareness by virtue of their linguistic ability to engage in inner speech. He concludes by presenting a table of the different types and categories of self-awareness to show what he believes animals are conscious of, and in doing so, provides a useful schema for showing that self-awareness exists on a gradient, from a basic awareness of one's own body, to a complex ability to take one's own self as an object of reflection for the purpose of self-evaluation (Morin 2012, pp. 255–256). In particular, Morin claims that while some animals are conscious of their own body and of being the agent behind their actions, they seem to be unaware of some private and public self aspects, such as physical appearance or attitudes. Some animals seem to know about their thoughts, and have the ability to mentally time travel. He even claims that some animals might be capable of less sophisticated forms of self-regulation and theory of mind, and although animals do not have linguistic capacities like those of humans, their less complex capacity for self-awareness is more directly related to a lack of inner speech. For Morin, the difference in levels of self-awareness between animals and humans is a matter of degree, and not of kind (2012, p. 256). This view not only supports the idea that self-awareness and selfhood exist at both minimal and complex levels, but it also supports the idea that animals are agents, as they are able to direct their own actions and learn from their subsequent effects. Although having a sense of agency seems somewhat ambiguous, it simply refers to the concept of self-awareness as something that accompanies the experience we have when we act. This level of self-awareness does not require any sort of complex reflection on the self, and so we can say that any animal that acts intentionally, or any minimal agent, is also at least minimally self-aware.

Colin McGinn (1995) argues in favour of selfhood in animals in a similar way to Zahavi, by maintaining the view that experiences cannot exist without a subject that unifies them. Selfhood from this point of view is simply the precondition for all conscious experience. As such, it is not available to us as an object to be examined directly, or as a specific kind of experience, but it is a conceptual necessity to make sense of conscious experiences. I agree with his claim, as when referring to work by Frege, McGinn says:

> Experience can never exist as a simple unanalyzable quality. The experience is always for something that is not itself an experience. We have a dyadic structure, consisting of a subject and what that subject experiences. The subject is not represented in the content of experience, of course; it is rather a precondition of there being any experience at all. The self is what has the experience, not something that the experience is about. (1995, p. 2)

We must assume the existence of a self in order to speak about experiences, or else the experiences would not belong to anyone. Indeed, we could not even speak of them *as* experiences, without an experiencer. This minimal sense of selfhood is all that is required for experiences and interests to matter to an individual, and all that is needed to posit the existence of a self. This is a useful way of understanding the self, as it applies equally to small human children and those with intellectual disabilities. There is no good reason to exclude animals from the community of selves, if we believe that marginal humans belong to it, as in many cases animals possess greater degrees of selfhood and self-awareness than these human individuals. So the concept of minimal self-awareness as a feature of consciousness that accompanies all conscious experiences, is then helpful in supporting the idea that children, intellectually disabled or brain-damaged humans, as well as animals possess a sense of self. This is important if we take the goal of consistency in our treatment of others seriously, regardless of the species an individual belongs to.

McGinn (1995) argues further that although different species of animals may have different moral weight, depending on the complexity of selfhood, every experiencing organism belongs to the same category as a subject of consciousness. He says:

> People have slowly come to accept that animals have experiences, in just as robust a sense as we do, but they have been reluctant to grant selfhood to animals. Selfhood is the thing that is held to distinguish us from the beasts, to put us on a different moral plane. This matters morally because the primary object of moral respect is precisely the self—that to which experiences happen…The moral community is the community of selves, and animals belong to this just as much as humans. (1995, p. 2)

McGinn rejects common objections to such a minimal requirement for moral consideration, including the idea that only moral agents capable of reflection are morally significant. Even a minimal sense of selfhood indicates that an individual can experience pain and suffering, for example, and killing an animal is "snuffing out a self, not simply interrupting a sequence of connected experiences" (1995, p. 7). As I argue in Chap. 4, selfhood is a requirement for autonomy, and this is why we owe direct moral obligations to animals that possess a sense of self. For the ability to make free choices is something we value in ourselves, and as a result of this, we also value it in others who are capable of acting freely. If we see animals as individuals for whom subjective experiences can be good or bad, just like us, then we are motivated to empathize with them and treat them with respect, rather than as unfeeling objects that we can use merely as the means to our own ends.

An important implication of this view is addressed by Cavalieri and Miller (1999), who argue that the self is *prescriptive*, as every sentient being has an awareness of how things seem to them, as well as how things are going for them. They claim that just because animals are unable to express their mental states with language, it does not mean that they are lacking the mental states or subjectivity that humans possess. They acknowledge that it is more difficult to understand the subjectivity of animals than of humans, but that we have enough evidence to show that many animals (particularly social species) are perceptually conscious, and that this requires a sense of self. Social animals, as they must understand relational, predictive, and manipulative problems (within social groups or between predators and prey) display a theory of mind as, "we become selves as we come to recognize selves" (Cavalieri and Miller 1999, p. 4). As animals navigate their way through their environments, they make decisions based on their interests. And "interests bring an evaluative aspect of the self which adds to the descriptive one. But the root goes deeper than interests. Why would the self see the satisfaction of its interests as good and value it, if it did not value itself?" (Cavalieri and Miller 1999, p. 7) By not acknowledging the moral value of selfhood in animals, yet respecting it in humans, Cavalieri and Miller argue that we are simply being speciesist.

Being speciesist is immoral in the same way that being racist or sexist is immoral. Basically, it means placing the interests of one's own species above the interests of other species for no other reason than species membership. This view was made popular by Peter Singer (1975), who claimed that species is an arbitrary category with which to make moral distinctions if sentience is shared between the species in question, whose interests may be in conflict. It is similar to racism and sexism, in terms of denying moral consideration to others based on morally irrelevant features. Although Singer, as a utilitarian, focuses on the interests of individuals and sentience as mattering the most morally, Cavalieri and

Miller believe that selfhood must also be recognized as a morally relevant feature across species. So to deny that animals have selves would not only be empirically inaccurate, it would also be speciesist, and thus, morally wrong.

Although many contemporary moral philosophers have made room for the consideration of animal interests in their theories, they do not go far enough in respecting the selfhood of animals. This is mainly due to their acceptance of animal consciousness, but not animal selfhood. As I argue further in Chap. 4, the autonomy that accompanies selfhood requires that we respect every individual's choices to the greatest degree possible, out of respect for the individual, not just their interests. It tends to be the case that when we focus on the interests of an animal we can still justify our treating it as merely a means to our own end, and not as an individual deserving of being treated as an end-in-itself. Cavalieri and Miller (1999) would agree with my view as they conclude:

> But, insofar as the deep, unifying prescriptive aspect of the self is not recognized, nonhuman lives are seen as expendable, and nonhuman interests are seen in a fragmentary way, and are subjected to aggregative calculus without any side constraints in the form of basic protection from interference. In what has been aptly defined "utilitarianism for animals, Kantianism for humans" (Nozick 1974), while humans are emphatically seen as selves, the other animals are considered as mere receptacles of experiences which can be separately weighed and traded-off. In fact, one could say that for mainstream moral philosophy nonhumans, though conscious, have no self. (10)

Taking the animal self seriously means rejecting a utilitarian account of animal ethics that focuses only on the interests that animals possess, rather than animals themselves, as I argue further in Chap. 4. A Kantian account of the moral importance of selfhood and autonomy provides a solution to the problem raised by Cavalieri and Miller, as it can be argued that animals are ends-in-themselves in the same way that humans are, as I argue in Chap. 6. If we accept that animals are conscious and are also self-aware, then the moral significance of selfhood requires us to respect the autonomy that accompanies it.

The Ecological Self and Evolutionary Continuity

Another line of argumentation that provides evidence in support of selfhood in animals comes from evolutionary theory. The reasoning here is that differences in levels of consciousness and self-consciousness are matters of degree and not of kind. Self-awareness, as previously argued, is most complex in its human form, allowing for abstract mental representations of the self, I-ness, or personal identity and reflective thought. The cognitive capacities that give rise to this complex level of self-awareness in humans are also found in varying degrees in other animal species, and are best understood by examining the evolutionary mechanisms that selected for them. So, although there are some key evolutionary differences between humans and other animals that allow humans to reflect, think abstractly, and drastically alter their environment, these differences have arisen from shared cognitive capacities in earlier ancestors that have evolved in other non-human animal species. Selfhood, as it is fundamentally constituted by self-awareness and the mental capacities required for self-awareness, is then a feature of consciousness shared among many species, to a greater or lesser degree. Given the strength of evidence in support of animal consciousness, the burden of proof shifts to those who want to argue that consciousness is discontinuous between human and other animal species.

Donald R. Griffin (2001) argues that:

> In view of the likelihood that all or at least a wide range of animals experience some form of subjective conscious awareness, it is both more parsimonious and more plausible to assume that the difference between human and other brains and minds is the content of conscious experience. This content of consciousness, what one is aware of, surely differs both qualitatively and quantitatively by astronomical magnitudes. Rather than an absolute all-or-nothing dichotomy between human brains uniquely capable of producing conscious experience, on one hand, and all other brains that can never do so, on the other, this hypothesis is consistent with our general belief in evolutionary continuity. (18)

Griffin makes an important distinction in this passage regarding the question of animal consciousness. Rather than view the issue as one of whether or not animals are conscious or unconscious, he believes that the difference between humans and other species lies in the content of their conscious experiences. Griffin also argues that it is by virtue of this subjective consciousness that animals are capable of directing their own behaviours by planning and choosing what to do. He describes animals as actors rather than objects, as they can adjust their behaviours according to challenges and stimuli in their environments. Griffin cites research throughout his writings that focuses on understanding how animals direct their own behaviours, specific to their species, and believes that this research confirms that animals are subjectively conscious creatures. He focuses on research that studies animal communication, physiological evidence of brain structures in animals that are associated with consciousness, and versatile adaptation to environmental challenges as evidence for the evolutionary continuity of consciousness across species (Griffin 2001, pp. 17–19).

Derek Bickerton (2000) provides further support for the conscious continuity between animal species by addressing the issue of how similar humans are to other animals in terms of the capacities required for consciousness, and does so by looking for a factor X that would account for the cognitive differences between humans and animals. Bickerton believes that as the capacities for art, language, research, and so on are restricted to humans, this could pose a problem for the argument of an evolutionary continuity between humans and other animals. His response, however—after evaluating various possible options for factor X, including speech and language capacities, brain size, and intelligence—is that the only difference between humans and other animals is the former's ability to maintain trains of thought through time for longer periods than other animals. From this he concludes that differences in consciousness between humans and other animals must be very small, thus defending the view of evolutionary continuity in consciousness and self-awareness across species. He argues that:

> Apart from discursive consciousness and the reification of the self, it seems highly likely that our consciousness is identical with that of other animals.

That is, we would be subjectively aware of our experience in exactly the same way. Animals would be conscious of what philosophers call "qualia"—the redness of a rose, the sweetness of a lump of sugar—in just the same way that we are; they would experience pain, hunger, thirst just as we do; they would have a similar subjective experience of emotions like fear, anger, sorrow while the constant bombardment of sensory stimuli all animals receive and filter appropriately would appear to them (allowing for differences, in some cases, of sensory modalities) much as it does to us. If such is indeed the case, it would seem to have significant implications for the ways in which we feel about, and behave towards, other species. (Bickerton 2000, p. 869)

Not only does Bickerton's argument support the existence of selfhood in animals from an evolutionary perspective, but it also supports it by defining consciousness *as* phenomenal consciousness. The experience of emotions is morally important in our treatment of other humans, and if we share these subjective feelings with animals, then it also makes them morally relevant. In fact, selfhood in animals, as a shared feature of subjective consciousness with humans, would obligate us more strongly than most other theories of animal ethics, as I argue in Chap. 5.

Another argument that provides evidence for selfhood in animals is based on the study of the development of selfhood in humans, beginning with infants, and progressing to the fully developed self-concept in adults (which is also the I-ness described previously). George Butterworth (1999) describes this as a developmental-ecological perspective of the self. Most importantly, he claims that the perceptual self exists prior to the self-concept found in adults, and that it allows for a distinction between self and environment that corresponds to Neisser's (1991) model of self-knowledge, which identifies and explains the key components of selfhood. Butterworth argues that, "The mental reflective self is just one relatively late-developing component of self" (1999, p. 204). Although in this case Butterworth is referring to the reflective self as late-developing in terms of the life of a human, others have argued that the ability to form a reflective self is also late-developing from an evolutionary perspective. The early developmental stages of the self correspond to the two first levels of self-knowledge as described by Neisser which include: "1. The ecological self, which is directly perceived with respect to the physical environment. 2. The interpersonal self, also directly perceived, which depends on emotional and other species-specific forms of communication." (Butterworth 1999, p. 204) These two levels of self-knowledge correspond to a self-awareness that includes the simple perception of self as opposed to object, and the perception of self as opposed to another self. There are three more levels of self-knowledge in Neisser's model, which include: the extended self that relies on memory and anticipation of the future; the private self that is reflective of our own experiences; and the self concept that is a theory of self shaped by socio-political influences. As Neisser argues that these last three levels of self-knowledge require a mental representation of the self (as an object of reflection) Butterworth believes that animals are not capable of achieving these levels of self-knowledge.

Butterworth also states that, "The cognitive or reflective aspect of self acquires its principle of unity from the perceptual-ecological aspect of self which engages the world with a unitary sense of self-agency. Unity of self is not a 'delusory projection' but it is not purely cognitive either; such unity can be observed before it is reasonable to postulate any ability to reflect on experience." (1999, p. 206) The perceptual-ecological self can be compared to the core self previously described by Zahavi (2005), as it is a prereflective sense of self that grants a creature the ability to direct its own behaviours, and which allows us to infer that there is something it is like to be that creature. It also means that the self is not reducible to one key cognitive or mental capacity, but rather it is "dependent on the proprioceptive functions of the body, on social and affective experiences and on cognitive developmental processes" (1999, p. 210). Selfhood in animals is composed of the same features as selfhood in humans, and perhaps the only difference between the reflective and non-reflective selves found in Butterworth's theory can be explained by Bickerton's claim that humans are simply capable of maintaining coherent neural signals over longer periods of time. This difference would allow for the kinds of mental representations of the self that allow for the extended and private self, and the self concept that distinguishes humans from other animals. The minimal, or prereflective, self that Zahavi describes is morally important as it indicates that experiences happen to someone and, as such, they provide the basis of interests which can be thwarted or fulfilled and affected by the actions of others. There is, however, great resistance to acknowledging that animals are selves, and even those who accept that animals have experiences have denied selfhood to animals and maintained that only humans possess this mental feature. This indicates the reluctance to accept the moral consequences of including animals within the moral community with humans, as it would require quite drastic changes in the ways we treat animals.

Another way to understand the development of the self comes from a sociological view on the various ways that interactions with animals contribute to human selfhood. Leslie Irvine (2004) provides an account of a core self in animals that consists of agency, coherence, affectivity, and history. She argues that through interactions with animals, humans can develop their own sense of self, but that this requires an understanding and acknowledgement of the subjectivity of the animal and its own self-awareness. Her method is to examine the capacities that animals must have to engage with humans, and her research focuses on dogs and cats and their interactions with humans in the context of an animal shelter, and her own autoethnographic notes about her experiences with her own companion cats. One question she asks is, "how do animals differ from the other 'objects' in our environment that contribute to our sense of self?" (Irvine 2004, p. 8) She believes that the answer to this question lies in the subjective presence of the Other, as someone who has a mind, beliefs, and desires. It is through the recognition and acknowledgment of this subjective Other that its own sense of self, as well as our own, is confirmed. As we cannot rely on self-reports of animals to sense their subjective presence, we must rely instead on our indirect perceptions of their subjectivity during interactions with them. And so, Irvine offers an account of four self-experiences that allow us to recognize subjectivity in others, and argues that these can also be applied to animals, in terms of their ability to sense the subjectivity of the humans and other animals they interact with. Taken together, these four kinds of self-experience compose a core sense of self that Irvine claims is possessed by the dogs and cats that were studied (2004, p. 9).

The first self-experience is agency, which Irvine defines as the capacity for self-willed action. Agency implies subjectivity, having control over one's actions, and an awareness of the felt consequences of those actions.

One example of this in dogs is the ability to exercise self-control, and Irvine argues that this ability implies that the dog must have a sense of control over its own actions, by first having a sense of will or volition (2004, p. 10). As such, this sort of learnt self-control indicates a sense of self. The second self-experience is coherence, which is claimed to be what provides the boundaries of the self, or what gives agency somewhere to "live". This is evidenced by the ability of shelter animals to recognize other distinct individuals, and also by the act of hiding, which requires a sense of self as something that can be concealed from others. Coherence then refers to the idea that particular animals have their own unique personalities and characteristics that, put together, form a coherent whole, or individual self (Irvine 2004, pp. 11–12). Affectivity is the third self-experience, which refers to an animal's capacity for emotions that help make their subjectivity available to us. Emotions such as sadness, happiness, fear, or anger are observable in animals, and we tend to characterize individual animals as sweet or mellow. Just as we do with other humans, we can read the overall emotional characteristics of individual animals, and Irvine claims that this is because they are indicators of their core self rather than just expressions of particular emotions (2004, p. 13). Last, self-history is the self-experience of continuity, made possible through memory. As Irvine says:

> Anyone who has ever taken a dog or cat to a veterinarian knows that animals remember places. The cat who loves affection at home now hisses and scratches the vet's offending hand. Skeptics might say that the animal "just smells fear," thereby dismissing the reaction as instinctual. However, even if it were "only" instinct, the consistent ability to register a particular emotion in a particular setting nevertheless implies a sense of continuity. (2004, p. 14)

Although animals may not have a sense of yesterday or next week in the same way we do, they do have memories of what they have experienced in the past. In our own interactions with animals, the memories animals have give us a sense of them as having their own history. Irvine concludes that through our interactions with animals as subjective selves, we confirm our own sense of agency. In this way, both humans and animals can be seen to develop a sense of self by interacting with each other within relationships. On her account, the core self of animals is less complex than that of fully developed humans, but it still shows that it is only by virtue of both humans and animals possessing a self that we are able to share our thoughts and feelings with each other at all. Thoughts and feelings cannot be shared between a human and a tree, as a tree is not a conscious, self-aware individual in the way that animals are. Our relationships with objects are different from relationships with other selves, as the latter contribute to the development of our own self-awareness, whereas the former do not. Intersubjectivity requires self-awareness in both individuals, even if that self-awareness is minimal. Irvine's account of self-awareness and selfhood in animals, although not a scientific view in itself, clearly shows that we can also support the idea of animals possessing minimal self-awareness from a sociological and interactionist perspective.

Empirical Evidence for Selfhood in Animals

Evidence for selfhood in animals takes many different forms, and there is no single experiment or type of test that can be applied to animals to search for consciousness. No single cognitive capacity makes for a decisive distinction between an animal that possesses self-awareness and one that does not. Indeed, one individual within a species, or one specific species of dolphin among many may possess a cognitive capacity that allows them to use tools, and so we might not be justified in making generalizations about all individuals within a species or across species in terms of these capacities. The point is rather that the research presented here implies the possession of certain cognitive capacities in some animal individuals and species that we might not expect at first glance, and this provides support for the idea that self-awareness and agency exists on a gradient from less complex forms to those we have come to expect in humans. Just because certain species might pass self-recognition tests, for example, does not make them elite species of some kind, that render other species entirely bereft of self-awareness. It is simply one capacity out of a large range of possible capacities, which taken on its own can be seen as part of a self-awareness gradient that exists both within and across different species. In what follows, I examine a sample of the various kinds of evidence that lend support to the existence of a gradient of more or less complex forms of consciousness and self-awareness in animals.

Perhaps the most well known type of experiment designed to search for self-awareness in animals is the mirror self-recognition test, which was originally designed for use on chimpanzees. By placing a mark of rouge on anesthetized chimpanzees and then putting them in front of mirrors after awakening, the observer would see whether or not the animal would touch the reflection in the mirror or if it would touch its own head to examine the rouge mark. Animals that touch or attempt to touch the mark on their own bodies while watching themselves in a mirror are considered to have successfully passed the test, and are considered to be self-aware (Toda and Watanabe 2008). These tests have been performed on many other species, and only human children over the age of two (Toda and Watanabe 2008), dolphins (Reiss and Marino 2001; Martin and Psarakos 1995), elephants, great apes, and chimpanzees (Plotnik et al. 2006) have passed as self-aware species. However, one challenge posed by such tests is that animals from dissimilar species will require uniquely designed experiments to test for this ability. For example, as dolphins do not have arms or hands, it posed more of a challenge to interpret their behaviour after being "marked" as indicative of self-recognition during experiments (Marino et al. 1994). So, aside from the fact that these experiments do not provide an absolute standard for identifying selfhood, they are also difficult to design for and tailor to various species. Fortunately, they are not the only source of evidence for selfhood in animals.

Although there are many kinds of memory, the focus of many studies on animals relates specifically to episodic memory. This is described by Zhanna Reznikova (2007) as "the conscious recall of specific past experience" and she argues: "Thus, episodic memory provides information about the 'what' and 'when' of events (temporally dated experiences) and about 'where' they happened (temporal-spatial relations)...This suggests that episodic memory is critically dependent on the concept of self." (76). Animals, including cephalopods (octopuses and cuttlefish, in particular), food-storing birds such as scrub jays and the storing marsh tit, chimpanzees, rhesus monkeys and gorillas, some rodents (mice and rats), and dolphins have all demonstrated behaviours considered indicative of episodic memory (for examples see Genarro 2009; Hampton 2001). This is a particularly important mental capacity for supporting the existence of selfhood in animals, as it suggests that along with basic concepts of objects, comes an understanding of them as enduring through time. As Genarro (2009) suggests, "if a conscious organism can reidentify the same object at different times, then it implicitly understands itself as something which endures through time" (189). The ability to recall past experiences requires at least a minimal form of "mental time travel", which would suggest the possession of at least a minimal form of self-awareness.

Cows and pigs are not normally the subjects of studies on self-awareness, but Donald M. Broom (2014) provides an account of some research that supports the existence of self-awareness in these animals. One study he describes asks if animals can be aware of their own learning or achievement, and by monitoring the emotional responses of young cattle as they were learning a new task of opening a gate to obtain food by breaking a light beam with their noses, they observed what they called the eureka effect. This occurs when an animal successfully learns to achieve their goal, and is indicated by excited behaviours (such as jumping and bucking) and by an increased heart rate. Broom believes this indicates a high degree of self-awareness, as it requires an awareness of the self in relation to the world around it for the cattle to be able to negotiate the task presented (2014, p. 81). The excitement exhibited by the cattle at their own achievements shows an awareness of their own learning. In a different study on pigs, Broom describes the feeding strategy that allowed a pig to watch as another, subordinate pig find food. The dominant pig then proceeded to rob the subordinate pig of its find. Subordinate pigs that were able to observe food being hidden by a human refrained from going to the food if a dominant pig was present. These behaviours indicate, according to Broom, that they possessed concepts of each other as dominant or subordinate, and that they exerted self-control until it became possible to obtain food safely. Broom says: "They were aware of the likely consequences of their action and of the behaviour of another animal before it happened." (2014, p. 83) He suggests that conscious experiences, or awareness, are likely to be the result of evolutionary processes, and that "self-awareness is the cognitive process in an individual when it identifies and has a concept of its body or possessions as being its own so that it can discriminate these from non-self stimuli" (Broom

2014, p. 80). This definition, along with the evidence provided in these studies on cattle and pigs, supports the view of minimal selfhood as the kind of mine-ness or body-ness we examined above.

Although the definition of what counts as a tool has been debated among scientists studying animals, it is generally agreed that tool use involves intentional action, problem-solving skills, and an awareness of the purpose for which it is intended (See Griffin 2001). Reznikova (2007) explains that tools are different from artefacts, such as beaver dams and nests, as they require that the animal select, prepare, and understand the function of the objects they choose for their particular purpose. Both Reznikova (2007) and Griffin (2001) provide examples of many birds—such as blue jays, Darwin's finches, crows, ravens, marsh tits, rooks, and Egyptian vultures—that have been observed using tools for the purposes of gaining access to food, grooming feathers, for use as a hammer or a missile. They also refer to observations of rodents, sea otters, primates of various kinds, and elephants who have also been shown to use tools, mainly for gaining access to food, but also for such things as protecting sensitive body parts against sharp objects (like coral or walking on rocks), to play with, as weapons, or for simply prodding others into play. While tool use may seem to indicate the existence of very complex mental capacities that allow for the advanced ability of problem-solving, insects (such as ants and wasps), and crabs, have also used simple tools to ward off attackers or lure prey (Griffin 2001). This may make it seem absurd to suggest that tool use is linked to self-awareness, unless we consider that mental capacities differ among species according to the particular environment in which they live. So, while some insects are capable of using tools, they may not exhibit social behaviour, or the capacity for communication, all of which have been attributed to certain primates and dolphins, for example. I would argue that what this means is that the more particular mental capacities that a species possesses, as demonstrated by the kinds of evidence presented in this chapter, the more complex the sense of selfhood that species has when you combine them together into one individual. So, self-awareness is indicated not only by the possession of one mental capacity, such as the ability to use tools, but also by the existence of a combination of these capacities within one individual or among many within a species.

Communication among animals takes many different forms, depending on the species and its physical and behavioural traits. Communication is basically the exchange of information between sender and receiver, using behavioural or other signals. According to Reznikova (2007), animal communication performs multiple functions, including, "(1) to advertise individual identity, presence and behavioural predispositions; (2) to establish social hierarchies; (3) to synchronise the physiological states of a group during breeding seasons; (4) to monitor the environment collectively for dangers and opportunities; (5) to synchronise organized activities (migration, foraging)." (325). Rogers and Kaplan (1998) explain that these signals can be: olfactory (such as scent glands or specialized skin cells in fish); taste (such as cats, sheep and goats tasting urine); auditory (such as bird or primate vocalizations); or visual (such as gesturing, using body postures or making facial expressions) (9–15). Studying animal communication can provide important evidence in support of animal consciousness, as it indicates that animals understand both the situation they find themselves in as well as the concept of other minds. As communication provides benefits for animals (such as predator/prey interactions), those with more developed communication skills may have greater evolutionary success. This would explain the evolutionary success of humans, but it would also support the notion that the cognitive capacities underlying language and communication are simply more or less complex, rather than considering human language as a defining feature of humans (and thereby supporting the idea that only humans have thoughts and/or concepts).

There are too many specific examples of animal communication to provide here, but a few are worth mentioning. One distinction in studying animal communication is between human/animal experiments, where humans "train" animals to respond to cues, and the observations of animal communication in the wild. Perhaps most familiar to us are studies where experimenters have taught various primates to use sign language. It has been shown through numerous experiments that primates are not just imitating signs, but that they understand what they are saying (Reznikova 2007). Parrots have also been taught to use English, most notably the African grey, Alex, who learnt more than 100 words and demonstrated that he understood what he was saying by correctly responding to various questions, and by indicating his own preferences (like where to sit, or when to exercise, etc.). Irene Pepperberg (Pepperberg and Lynn 2000), who trained Alex, has argued that parrots with this ability are likely to be at least perceptually conscious in order to make correct associations between objects and words, and to answer questions correctly (in a statistically significant way) that they have not heard before. Experiments involving gaze-following in dogs and chimpanzees and human experimenters have shown an immediate grasp and understanding by these animals of human gestures as a form of communication (Barth et al. 2005; Soproni et al. 2001). Dolphins excel in understanding human language (usually an "artificial" language of gestures), and Thomas White (2007) claims that they understand the semantic and syntactic features of sentences. There are many more such examples of animal communication, and as the acceptance of intentional behaviours in animals increases, so too does the scientific study of animal communication in other species. This is significant, for in the past, many scientists were hesitant to label animal signals and communication as intentional. Acceptance of these claims indicates a wider acknowledgement of animal consciousness and self-awareness within the scientific community (Rogers and Kaplan 1998). Since communication between individuals presupposes at least a minimal recognition of a distinction between self and other, it is a useful indicator of the possession of beliefs and an awareness of oneself. Marc Bekoff (2006a, b) and others (Cheney and Seyfarth 2007; Griffin 2001) point to the abilities of social animals to play, deceive, and imitate others as evidence of possessing a sense of other minds, and in some cases of time, of the world around them and the choices it presents to them, as evidence of self-awareness. Animals may not be able to rationally reflect on these experiences or analyze them as humans do, but they must have varying degrees of self-awareness that allow them to make decisions based on their own beliefs, concepts, desires, and goals.

Objections to Selfhood in Animals

Mirror self-recognition tests are looking for a concept of self within humans and animals, but for not a self as such. That is, these tests are looking for I-ness, or self-identity, in terms of a creature being able to take itself as an object of reflection. Mine-ness, I believe, means that a creature does have a sense of self, but it may not be able to take that self as an object of its own reflection. This is an important distinction to make, because some have denied the existence of an animal self that is based on the animal's ability to pass the mirror self-recognition test successfully. Indeed, the debate between Povinelli and Gallup (1998) rests on this distinction. Gallup argues that if an animal passes this test, it has a self, including a self-concept of itself and others or, in other words, a theory of mind. Povinelli argues that even if an animal passes this test, it does not settle either the question of the animal having a self at all, or the animal having a self-concept. I do not believe that either view is entirely correct. The mirror self-recognition tests only indicate the level of self-awareness that an animal has (and even this is hotly debated), but it does not determine whether an animal has a self at all. Failure to pass these tests successfully does not indicate that an animal does not have a self, just as passing the test does not necessarily establish that an animal is successfully or explicitly identifying itself. If these tests are taken along with other studies and observations of animal behaviour in a cumulative fashion, then inferences based on them are sufficient to establish that animals do have a sense of self, even if minimally so.

Povinelli (1998) argues that a theory of mind is required for a self-concept. Possessing a theory of mind means that a creature has a form of self-awareness that allows it to make inferences about the mental state of itself and others. As the mental states of others are not directly observable, the creature in question must have a "theory" about the mental states of others in order to make predictions about their behaviours (Povinelli 1998, p. 50). Self-recognition tests have been used as a general standard to determine whether or not an animal can recognize itself as distinct from others. While Gallup and others have argued that various species, such as certain primates, dolphins, and elephants, have successfully passed these sorts of tests (as described in an earlier section of this chapter), implying that these animals have a theory of mind, Povinelli and others have argued that the results have been misinterpreted for various reasons, and that these animals do not have a theory of mind (1998, pp. 51–52). Without going into great detail, it is clear that the issue of whether or not an animal can identify itself as distinct from another, and even make inferences about the mental states of others, can be resolved through means other than the mirror-recognition tests seen to be the hallmark of identifying a self-concept in animals. That is, a theory of mind is not required for an animal to have a sense of what it is like to be that animal, or a phenomenal self. These experiments are important for determining the details of the cognitive processes in humans and animals, but are not the standard we should use in determining whether or not an animal has a self-concept at all.

There are those who argue that even if animals do have emotions and feelings, we could not possibly know if they are the same emotions and feelings that we experience. Indeed, a stronger version of this argument is that to "place" emotions and feelings on animals is inaccurate and misleading, to the extent that it may even be harmful to the animals themselves if we base our treatment of them on this knowledge. That is, if we are mistaken in our assumptions about the feelings of animals and their experiences, it could lead to interactions with them that could cause them more pain and suffering, even if that is what we are seeking to avoid in the first place. de Waal (1999) says that "the original meaning of anthropomorphism is that of misattribution of human qualities to nonhumans, or at least overestimation of the similarities between humans and nonhumans. Since nobody wants to be accused of any type of misattribution or overestimation, this makes it sound as if anthropomorphism is to be avoided under all circumstances." (256). Scientists in particular, whose aim at objectivity in research and knowledge is justifiably of utmost importance, are wary of the threat of anthropomorphism when studying and interpreting the behaviours of animals. Griffin (1999) claims: "In scientific usage anthropomorphism means the assertion that a nonhuman organism displays some attribute or behaviour that is in fact uniquely human." (236) He says that his own research into animal consciousness has evoked "vigorous criticisms" from behavioural scientists, including having one of his own books "likened to Salmon Rushdie's *Satanic Verses.*" (237). He wonders why it is generally acceptable to perform research as biologists on such topics as comparative mammalian anatomy, disease, and physiology, but not acceptable to perform research as ethologists into animal consciousness and behaviour. He says: "Subjective experience is almost the only attribute that has remained immune from recognition of evolutionary continuity." (238) This is very telling as to the importance of selfhood in animals in the development of an animal ethic, as it is what allows us to consider an animal as some*one* rather than simply some*thing*. The threat of anthropomorphism to the objectivity and accuracy of research on animal minds points directly to the moral importance of the acceptance of the selfhood of animals, constituted mainly by the phenomenal aspects of what it is like to be an animal.

Griffin (1999) points out that many have argued that this concern about overestimating the mental capacities in animals is a result of the acceptance of the behaviourist influence on psychology, whereby Morgan's Canon serves to suppress studies of animal behaviour that use "introspective and subjectivistic approaches" (258). This is because Morgan's Canon states: "In no case may we interpret an action as the outcome of the exercise of a higher psychical faculty, if it can be interpreted as the outcome of the exercise of one which stands lower on the psychological scale." (Griffin 1999, p. 258) This canon is intended to prevent anthropomorphism from occurring when one interprets observed animal behaviours, by favouring the underestimation of the mental complexity of animals giving rise to those behaviours. However, could it not be argued that it is equally wrong to overestimate the mental capacities of humans, or that it is in fact better to overestimate than underestimate the mental capacities of non-humans? To underestimate the mental capacities of non-humans is also to deny the evolutionary continuity of consciousness that is held in widespread agreement among many scientists. As previously argued, there are good reasons for using the evolutionary continuity of consciousness to support the existence of self-awareness and selfhood in animals. There is no good reason to deny that animals have a subjective, phenomenal awareness of their experiences, except perhaps for the fear of the moral implications that would result. In a book entirely devoted to the study of corvids, Marzluff and Angell (2012) present research and observations about the complexity of behaviours and mental capacities in birds. They argue that:

> Understanding the mentality of other animals is in its infancy. And as with all our views on nature, we can assemble it only from our human perspective. We may never know what crows think about, but by understanding more about the anatomy, chemistry, and physics of their brains, we are learning something about how they may think. We may not, in this way, truly understand the mind of the crow, but we can begin to understand the

brain of the crow. The glimpse we have revealed suggests that crows possess a brain capable of complex thought, which is consistent with an advanced state of conscious awareness. These animals, which we often take for granted and aggressively combat, really are thinking and reasoning in ways that are more similar to our own than many would care to admit. (Marzluff and Angell 2012, pp. 197–198)

Despite the fact that we are limited to examining the minds of animals from our own human perspective, it is possible to gain knowledge and understanding of their mental capacities through careful observation and by applying what we know from various areas of science to the brains of animals. Marzluff and Angell point out our hesitation in admitting to the complexity of the minds of birds, as they believe it challenges our thinking about how we interact with them on a moral level. Studying the minds of animals not only challenges our scientific views, but also challenges our moral beliefs and how we understand our own place, alongside other animals, within nature.

Another concern with anthropomorphism is the more general problem of access to other minds. It could be argued that we never really gain knowledge of what it is like to be another person, let alone an animal whose species-specific body and senses are so different from ours, that we would have an even wider experience to bridge. Granted, we may never know exactly what it is like to be a lion, whale, or bat, but that does not preclude us from accepting that there is something it is like to be one of those animals. Just as we must infer from the behaviours of other humans what it is like to be them, we must make inferences about the experiences of animals based on their behaviours. That is not to say that we are unable to do this in a careful, respectful way, that acknowledges and takes into consideration the differences and similarities between us and those we are studying. In fact, we are unable not to anthropomorphize, as we are limited by our own experiences and perspectives when we observe the behaviours of those around us. The careful use of anthropomorphism can be useful in science to frame investigations and explanations of observations of animal behaviours. de Waal (1999) suggests an "heuristic anthropomorphism" as a scientific model for the interpretation of data. This model legitimates the use of anthropomorphism as a useful perspective from which to make "guesses" that will inform hypotheses regarding the function of an animal's behaviour. In this way, we can continue to gain evidence to support the existence of selfhood and consciousness in animals through observation and experimentation.

Conclusion

In this chapter I have argued for a concept of selfhood that ranges from minimal to more complex levels self-awareness. This is supported by arguments based on the nature of phenomenal consciousness, the evolutionary continuity of species, and scientific research into animal minds. It is also supported by a sociological model that posits a core self that animals possess and that is recognizable through interactions with them. Despite disagreements regarding definitions of selfhood and sceptical views on the interpretation of animal behaviour, the view that animals are conscious and experience subjective mental states is clearly supported when we take the evidence for it as a whole.

Along with this I present reasons why selfhood in animals is morally important, and I support this further in subsequent chapters, where I claim that autonomy can be understood as accompanying selfhood, and that we owe all creatures respect for that autonomy, even if it exists in only a minimal sense.

References

Allen, Colin, "Animal Consciousness", The Stanford Encyclopedia of Philosophy (Winter 2011 Edition), Edward N. Zalta (ed.), http://plato.stanford.edu/archives/win2011/entries/consciousnessanimal.

Barth, J., Reaux, J.E., & Povinelli, D.J. (2005). Chimpanzees' (Pan troglodytes) use of gaze cues in object-choice tasks: different methods yield different results. Animal Cognition, 8, 84–92.

Bekoff, M. (2003). Considering animals—Not "higher" primates: Consciousness and self in animals: Some reflections. *Zygon, 38*(2), 229–245.

Bekoff, Marc and Paul W. Sherman. (2004). Reflections on animal selves. Trends in Ecology and Evolution. Vol. 19, No. 4, 176–180.

Bekoff, M. (2006a). Animal emotions and animal sentience and why they matter: Blending 'science sense' with common sense, compassion and heart. In

J. Turner & J. D'Silva (Eds.), *Animals, ethics and trade: The challenge of animal sentience* (pp. 27–40). London: Earthscan.
Bekoff, M. (2006b). *Animal passions and beastly virtues: Reflections on redecorating nature.* Philadelphia: Temple University Press.
Bickerton, D. (2000). Resolving discontinuity: A minimalist distinction between human and non-human minds. *American Zoologist, 40*(6), 862–873.
Broom, D. M. (2014). *Sentience and animal welfare.* Boston: CABI.
Butterworth, G. (1999). A developmental-ecological perspective on Strawson's 'the self'. In S. Gallagher & J. Shear (Eds.), *Models of the self* (pp. 203–211). Thorverton: Imprint Academic.
Cavalieri, P., & Miller, H. B. (1999). Automata, receptacles, and selves. *Psyche, 5*(24), 1–13.
Cheney, D. L., & Seyfarth, R. M. (2007). *Baboon metaphysics: The evolution of a social mind.* Chicago: The University of Chicago Press.
Dawkins, M. S. (2012). *Why animals matter: Animal consciousness, animal welfare and human well-being.* Toronto: Oxford University Press.
DeGrazia, David. (2009). Self-awareness in animals. In Lurz, Robert W. (Ed.) The Philosophy of Animal Minds. New York: Cambridge University Press, 201–217.
de Waal, F. B. M. (1999). Anthropomorphism and anthropodenial: Consistency in our thinking about humans and other animals. *Philosophical Topics, 27*(1), 255–280.
Griffin, D. R. (1999). Nonhuman minds. *Philosophical Topics, 27*(1), 233–254.
Griffin, D. R. (2001). *Animal minds: Beyond cognition to consciousness.* Chicago: The University of Chicago Press.
Hampton, R. R. (2001). Rhesus monkeys know when they remember. *Proceedings of the National Academy of Sciences in the United States of America, 98*(9), 5359–5362.
Irvine, L. (2004). A model of animal selfhood: Expanding interactionist possibilities. *Symbolic Interaction, 27*(1), 3–21.
Martin, K., & Psarakos, S. (1995). Evidence of self-awareness in the bottlenose dolphin (Tursiops truncatus). In S. T. Parker, R. W. Mitchell, & M. L. Boccia (Eds.), *Self-awareness in animals and humans: Developmental perspectives* (pp. 361–379). New York: Cambridge University Press.
Marzluff, J., & Angell, T. (2012). *Gifts of the crow: How perception, emotion, and thought allow smart birds to behave like humans.* Toronto: Free Press.
McGinn, C. (1995). Animal minds, animal morality. *Social Research, 62*(3), 1–8.

Morin, A. (2012). What are animals conscious of? In J. A. Smith & R. W. Mitchell (Eds.), (2012). *Experiencing animal minds: An anthology of animal-human encounters* (pp. 246–260). New York: Columbia University Press.

Nagel, T. (1979). What is it like to be a bat? *The Philosophical Review, 83*(4), 435–450.

Neisser, U. (1991). Five kinds of self-knowledge. In D. Kolak & R. Martin (Eds.), *Self and identity: Contemporary philosophical issues* (pp. 386–403). Toronto: Collier Macmillan Canada.

Pepperberg, I. M., & Lynn, S. K. (2000). Possible levels of animal consciousness with reference to grey parrots. *American Zoologist, 40*(6), 893–901.

Plotnik, J., de Waal, F. B., & Reiss, D. (2006). Self-recognition in an Asian elephant. *Proceedings of the National Academy of Sciences of the United States of America, 103*(45), 17053–17057.

Povinelli, D. J. (1998). When self met other. In M. Ferrari & R. J. Sternberg (Eds.), *Self-awareness: Its nature and development* (pp. 37–107). New York: Guilford.

Reiss, D., & Marino, L. (2001). Mirror self-recognition in the bottlenose dolphin: A case of cognitive convergence. *Proceedings of the National Academy of Sciences of the United States of America, 98*(10), 5937–5942.

Reznikova, Z. (2007). *Animal intelligence: From individual to social cognition*. New York: Cambridge University Press.

Rogers, L. J. (1997). *Minds of their own: Thinking and awareness in animals*. Australia: Allen & Unwin.

Rogers, L. J., & Kaplan, G. (1998). *Not only roars & rituals: Communication in animals*. Australia: Allen & Unwin.

Soproni, K., Miklosi, A., Topal, J., & Csanyi, V. (2001). Comprehension of human communicative signs in pet dogs. *Journal of Comparative Psychology, 115*(2), 122–126.

Toda, Koji and Shigeru Watanabe. (2008). Discrimination of moving video images of self by pigeons (Columba livia). Animal Cognition, 11, 699–705.

White, T. I. (2007). *In defense of dolphins: The new moral frontier*. Malden: Blackwell Publishing.

Zahavi, D. (2005). *Subjectivity and selfhood: Investigating the first-person perspective*. Cambridge: The MIT Press.

4

Autonomy and Animals

Introduction

In Chaps. 2 and 3 I argued that agency and selfhood are features of conscious animals, and that these capacities exist at more and less complex levels depending on the mental capacities found in different species and individual animals. I also argued that agency and selfhood are morally valuable as they indicate a subject for whom experiences matter. But we need more explanation as to why we ought to respect agency and selfhood in animals, and how we can do this. Autonomy, as a moral concept, best fits with my view on agency and selfhood as it requires respect not only for someone's interests, but also for the individual as the one who experiences the thwarting or fulfilment of those interests. Just as I argued that agency and selfhood can be more or less complex, so too can autonomy exist in varying degrees.

That is not to say that the various conceptions of autonomy accepted by most people are not important, or that there are levels of autonomy that are not uniquely human. The attempt to achieve "authenticity" or "heroic" autonomy is a human quest, and a worthy one. But if autonomy ranges from self-governance over our most basic actions to a complex notion of authenticity, then the concept clearly admits to existing in degrees. A person who is intellectually disabled is autonomous, but not to the same level of complexity as someone who reads Spinoza in an attempt to achieve greater authenticity. However, in my view, each level of autonomy is equally valuable in terms of the moral obligations owed to each person or individual.

I will support this view by first considering what I call the common view of autonomy, whereby only normal, adult humans are considered autonomous persons. After pointing out the problems with this conception of autonomy, I posit the view that autonomy can exist at both rich, human levels and more minimal, animal and "marginal human", levels. We simply owe individuals respect for their autonomy to the extent that they are self-aware. I explain how moral duties are founded on the concept of autonomy, by including an analysis of Gewirth's argument on this subject. I also consider other views of autonomy that complement my own, and that challenge the common view to show that although not widely popular, accounts of a more minimal autonomy in animals are plausible and well supported.

The Common View of Autonomy

Autonomy is a commonly used moral concept with which to judge our treatment of others. In medicine, for example, we use the concept of autonomy to help determine if someone has made an informed and free decision regarding a prescribed treatment or procedure. We shun overly paternalistic models of professional physician–patient relationships because we believe that significant harms can result from overriding a patient's freedom of choice, in terms of decisions regarding their own treatment. Autonomy also guides us in our personal relationships with others, and provides us with a measure of how we ought to treat our friends, family members, and partners. "Good" relationships are usually judged by the level of respect each member has for the other, to allow for the maximal personal fulfilment of each person. We also believe that to respect someone else means to also respect their autonomy, as personhood implies certain faculties and characteristics that allow one control over their own actions and decisions. In a moral sense, we want to respect the autonomy of others because we want the same respect to be given to us. Just as we value our own freedom to act in accordance with our desires and preferences, so too do we value the same freedom in others. Generally speaking, we refer to this sort of freedom as autonomy.

Gerald Dworkin (1988) describes the various meanings of autonomy in the following passage:

> It is sometimes used as an equivalent of liberty (positive or negative in Berlin's terminology), sometimes as equivalent to self-rule or sovereignty, sometimes as identical with freedom of the will. It is equated with dignity, integrity, individuality, independence, responsibility, and self-knowledge. It is identified with qualities of self-assertion, with critical reflection, with freedom from obligation, with absence of external causation, with knowledge of one's own interests. It is even equated by some economists with the impossibility of interpersonal comparisons. It is related to actions, to beliefs, to reasons for acting, to rules, to the will of other persons, to thoughts, and to principles. About the only feature held constant from one author to another are that autonomy is a feature of persons and that it is a desirable quality to have. It is very unlikely that there is a core meaning which underlies all these various uses of the term. (6)

Of particular importance in this passage is Dworkin's claim that the two constant features of autonomy are that of personhood, and that it is a desirable quality to have. It is also significant that he claims that autonomy defies a core meaning. In other words, there are many different definitions of autonomy, which allow for ample debate on the topic. Generally, personhood is related to autonomy as a way of delineating those who are owed direct moral obligations from those who are not, and this would distinguish humans as persons from non-human animals, who are generally not considered to be full persons. As such, it gives us a neat classification between someone and something, where to the latter we may owe indirect moral duties, as in Kant's theory for how we ought to treat animals (in Chap. 6 I present an account of this). Autonomy as a desirable quality to have can be understood as our desire to act freely, in order to fulfil our interests and preferences. The freedom to do so allows us to achieve the fulfilment of what we believe is good for us, or makes us happy and satisfied. To act without autonomy is to be manipulated, coerced, or forced to act against our own will, which can result in various harms, including frustration and suffering.

Without a core meaning, it can be difficult to narrow down why autonomy is such a desired feature. But if we think about the role that autonomy plays in moral theory, we can argue that it is valuable as it represents the ability people have to direct their own actions independently from the influence of others. That is, autonomy basically means being able to make one's own decisions, for one's own reasons. And autonomy provides us with a moral and political standard to guide us in determining appropriate ways to interact with each other. Although it would be impossible to make decisions entirely without the influence of others, autonomy allows us to control everything from our most basic actions to those that reflect our grandest future goals or desires for self-improvement or self-fulfilment. Moral theories and laws protect this ability or freedom we have by elaborating on the ways we can best exercise and develop it through our relationships with others, individually and within society as a whole.

Even without a definitive or core concept of autonomy, it is possible to narrow down some of its basic features to better clarify who possesses it. Nomy Arpaly (2003) analyzes the concept of autonomy and argues that people commonly refer to roughly eight different kinds of autonomy, which I have summarized as:

1. Agent autonomy. This refers to the agent's ability to choose between various motivational states, and can be equated with self-control or self-governance.
2. Personal efficacy-material independence. This is the general ability to get along in the world without help, in material matters.
3. Personal efficacy-psychological independence. This is the general ability to get along in the world without help in psychological matters.
4. Normative, moral autonomy. This is the freedom to make one's own decisions and the freedom from paternalistic intervention.
5. Authenticity. This refers to the idea of being true to oneself (Frankfurt), and that there is a real self or personal identity.

6. Self-identification. This is described as someone who has a harmonious and coherent self-image, who never experiences her desires as an external threat.
7. Heroic autonomy. These are ideal concepts of autonomy, such as Spinoza's freedom, Aristotle's life of contemplation, Freud's or Jung's idea of liberation, and Nietzsche's ideal of free spirit.
8. Response to reasons. This is the kind of autonomy that allows one to act rationally and to respond to moral reasons and reasons in general, and includes Kant's concept of rational autonomy. (Arpaly 2003, pp. 119–126)

This sketch of the different kinds of autonomy emphasizes that there are different perspectives on how to define the concept, and some of these kinds overlap in various ways. They are all, however, examples of what I take to be the common view of autonomy, as they are all generally applicable to humans only. Indeed, Arpaly argues that none of the conceptions of autonomy listed above properly apply to non-human animals, as she endorses the agent-autonomy view, which requires that an agent can decide on which of her motivational states she wants to follow (2003, p. 118). She believes that autonomy at any level requires a certain degree of reflection and deliberation that animals do not have, as they are unable to act as a result of moral reasons. That is not to say that animals never act as a result of reasons of any kind, but as they do not act from moral reasons, they should not be included as autonomous creatures. For her, there may be other reasons for treating animals morally, but they are not related to autonomy (2003, pp. 145–148). As we saw in Chap. 2, there are arguments that challenge this view based on the idea that animals can act on the basis of moral reasons, such as that made by Rowlands (2012). For Arpaly, as an example of the common view of autonomy, the ability to act morally is a fundamental part of what it means to act autonomously. This is because, as pointed out by Rowlands (2012), moral agency is generally understood to be necessarily connected to moral responsibility, and as we cannot hold animals responsible for their actions some might thereby discount them as autonomous, insofar as they are not viewed as moral agents. It is important to pull apart these notions to better clarify the differences between them. Agency, for example, does not necessarily imply moral agency, and autonomy does not necessarily imply moral responsibility. From a common view of autonomy however, these implications are often drawn, and it is due to these implications that animals are so often denied as autonomous on any level.

This means that discussions on the importance of autonomy tend to assume that only humans are autonomous agents by virtue of their rational capacities to reflect on their goals, desires, and decisions. Rachels and Ruddick (1989), for example, assume that autonomy requires a capacity for high-level mental representations, memory, and imagination that allow a person to both remember their past and anticipate their future. Only under these conditions can free choices be made, according to many. Although there is no consensus on the meaning or conditions of autonomy, it is described in such a way as to fit the purpose of the moral argument it is found within. The following describes perhaps the most common understanding of autonomy, as explained by David Richards (1989):

> Autonomy, in the sense fundamental to the idea of human rights, is a complex assumption about the capacities, developed or undeveloped, of persons, which enable them to develop, want to act on, and act on higher-order plans of action which take as their self-critical object one's life and the way it is lived. As Frankfurt put it, persons "are capable of wanting to be different, in their preferences and purposes, from what they are. Many animals appear to have the capacity for…'first-order desires' or 'desires of the first order,' which are simple desires to do or not do one thing or another. No animal other than man, however, appears to have the capacity for reflective self-evaluation that is manifested in the formation of second-order desires." These capacities enable persons to establish various kinds of priorities and schedules for the satisfaction of first-order desires. (205)

Animals are denied autonomy in this account as they are believed to lack the ability for reflective evaluation of their actions and choices. They are seen to act only on the basis of first-order desires, and not on second-order desires which consist of the ability to reflect on and evaluate their first-order desires. Instead, most would describe animals as acting on instinct without the ability to regulate their own behaviours. This makes sense given a history of science that, for many years, denied that animals had the ability to think or feel. Although many people would be hesitant now to deny animals these abilities, there is still a great reluctance to attribute intentional mental states to animals or the capacity for autonomous action. But if autonomous action is seen simply as the freedom to act on the basis of reasons, however minimally complex they might be, then autonomy does exist at the level of first-order desires. Besides, as Rowlands (2012, pp. 178–180) argues, to claim that there is something about second-order desires that magically allows an individual to overcome the motivational power of first-order desires is mistaken, as there is nothing about second-order desires that grants greater control over one's actions than those of the first-order. This challenges the common view of autonomy as it means that the ability to reflect rationally on our reasons for acting does not make us more autonomous, in terms of moral agency. It does not however, preclude the idea that autonomy can simply be understood as the ability to act on the basis of reasons, such as beliefs, desires, and preferences, even if these are minimally complex. Part of the resistance to accepting a view of autonomy is that, because of the common connection between personhood and autonomy, and the connection between personhood and legal rights, the consequences of accepting animals as autonomous would have profound effects on the ways we treat and legislate protection for animals. This means that we often overlook the possibility that animals can share in the possession of such a feature with us, in a more minimal way, preferring to understand the issue as one of a difference in kind.

While it is reasonable to claim that many humans possess autonomy in a rich sense, which includes life goals and the ability to reflect on one's own desires, it does not mean, as I have argued above, that autonomy does not exist in a more minimal sense among animals. R. G. Frey (1987) argues that the attempts that have been made to include beings other than humans in the moral class of autonomy illustrates the moral privilege that we associate with being autonomous. Although Frey does not endorse cruelty towards animals, he believes that autonomy is irrelevant in explaining why we should avoid causing animals suffering, and that animals are not autonomous in any way. He does believe that autonomy indicates the value of a life, and so when it comes to killing, the fact that animals are not autonomous (according to him) is relevant, as it means that "the threshold for killing animals is lower than that for killing normal humans" (Frey 1987, p. 51). After admitting that autonomy is understood in many different ways, he endorses a view he calls "autonomy as control", which focuses on being able to control our first-order desires in an attempt to shape our own lives in accordance with our conception of the good life. In describing this view, he writes that autonomy as control is valuable:

> For it enables us to live our lives as we see fit and to make of them what we will; it becomes, then, a means to that rich full life of self-fulfillment and achievement, quite apart from any satisfaction and fulfillment that comes through the satisfaction of our appetites, that so separates men from animals. When we look back and say of a human being that he led a rich, full life, we allude to something incomparably beyond that to which we would allude, were we to say the same thing of a chicken or a dog. And autonomy is a key to this notion of a life of accomplishment and self-fulfillment, lived according to one's conception of the good life (Frey 1987, p. 54).

For Frey, only full persons are autonomous, and so infant humans and those who are "seriously defected", along with animals, are excluded from this moral category. In fact, his claim is that those people who are autonomous have more value, or moral weight, than those who do not. As such, he is very much in opposition to animal rights or the comparison of animals to humans on egalitarian grounds, as he maintains a strict division between autonomous and non-autonomous beings. However, if we consider the idea that many humans are not fully autonomous, such as addicts or the mentally ill, does that push them out of the autonomous category, or does it just make them less autonomous than those who are more rational? It is not clear why his view of autonomy as control is more valuable than, say, the preference autonomy view of Tom Regan (1983). It also seems that, despite his emphasis on autonomy as an all-or-nothing category, this simply is not the case for humans if, by his own argument, entire categories of humans can also be discounted as autonomous.

The important question raised by all of this is whether or not some forms of autonomy are more important or valuable than others? Are our moral obligations greater towards those who possess the ability to achieve personal authenticity, than those who are simply capable of something like personal efficacy? What reasons might we have for valuing some forms of autonomy over others? It is not clear from what we have examined above how each form of autonomy ought to be valued, or to what extent it ought to be respected. It simply lays out, more specifically, the ways that people have conceived of freedom and autonomy in various philosophical views, and emphasizes the common view that humans are unique as autonomous beings.

Minimal Autonomy

Notions of autonomy quite often represent what are considered to be the distinguishing and unique features of human nature, which include a complex level of rational, reflective thought, higher order desires to shape ourselves into morally virtuous people, and the freedom to act as a result of our "true" selves. This rich view of autonomy grants humans special moral status, as agents who can freely choose among alternative possibilities and who are responsible for their actions. Most animals would clearly not count as autonomous on this view.

But, I propose that just as there are both rich and basic levels of self, so too are there rich and basic levels of autonomy. These different levels of autonomy result in different kinds of moral treatment. If we only assume the rich level of autonomy, which is characterized as reflective, rational thought, then the majority of animals would remain outside the scope of moral concern. What I am arguing for here is a more basic level of autonomy, that correlates with the basic level of self-awareness that I presented in Chap. 3. It is by virtue of this basic level of autonomy that we have moral obligations towards animals. The degree to which a being is autonomous ought to be respected as fully as possible, and the degree to which a being is self-aware indicates how autonomous it is. Specific traits and interests would vary according to species membership, and we would need to evaluate species individually to determine the level of autonomy possessed by an individual and the ways we can best respect it.

Steven M. Wise (2002) has made one such attempt to support the notion of degrees of autonomy by creating a "scale of practical autonomy", where one can assign "autonomy values" to animals by creating four categories, each of which requires a different level of moral and legal treatment. He posits that "practical autonomy" entails basic liberty rights when a creature can desire, can try to fulfil its desires through intentional action, and possesses an awareness, even minimally, of itself and that its desires belong to it. Consciousness and sentience are required to possess practical autonomy, but no level of reflective evaluation of one's preferences is needed. In Category One, he places animals that are self-aware and that can pass mirror self-recognition tests, as he believes this justifies the claim that they have part or all of a theory of mind, and that "they understand symbols, use a sophisticated language or language-like communication system, and may deceive, pretend, imitate, and solve complex problems (Wise 2002, p. 36). Category Two includes animals that have a simpler sense of self, and who can make simple choices from among their options for acting. This category is broad, and animals within this category will have varying liberty rights (in terms of strength) based on taxonomic class and "the nearness of her evolutionary relationship to humans" (Wise 2002, p. 37). Whether animals are placed in Category Two is dependent on their mental and cognitive capacities. Category Three includes animals that we do not know enough about to dismiss as conscious, and Category Four includes animals that we believe lack all consciousness, and who are remote from humans on a taxonomic and evolutionary scale (Wise 2002, p. 37). This view includes provisions for a wide range of animals and it errs on the side of caution when research on specific mental capacities is lacking among certain species.

Although Wise makes this particular argument to support the idea of legal rights for animals, it is useful for highlighting the relationship between consciousness and autonomy and the idea that they exist to varying degrees in animals. There is no denying that humans can have a more complex level of autonomy, which includes such things as life plans and future goals, or fully-fledged moral agency. However, as Wise points out, many humans do not act as a result of rational reflection and, what I have called, the common conception of autonomy. It is very difficult to claim that humans act as a result of reason and not desire, and in the courtroom, according to Wise: "Judges accept the nonrational determination of Jehovah's Witnesses to die rather than accept blood transfusions. The mentally ill are not usually confined against their wishes unless they pose a threat to themselves or others." (Wise 2002, p. 31) As such, Wise claims, the reality for moral and political philosophers, as for judges, is that "lesser autonomies" do exist, and all that is required of someone to be considered autonomous is the ability to make choices and to act in ways that aim to satisfy her own desires and preferences. This is true even if the person is unable to rationally evaluate their own choices, or evaluate them very well.

Autonomy can be taken to mean the freedom to direct one's actions towards attaining goods recognized as such by a self-aware creature. Self-awareness is what allows a creature to recognize things that matter to itself. It is by virtue of having a self, in terms of having a self-directedness, that a creature can direct its own actions and intentions towards attaining certain goals. The importance of autonomy for animal ethics is that it indicates the need to consider how we can respect both positive and negative freedoms. According to moral theories in general, ensuring the absence of pain or suffering is not enough because autonomy also asks us to consider the positive freedoms of an individual. This means, according to some, like Rogers and Kaplan (2004), that a creature deserves to "have a quality of life commensurate with their needs and dignity: physical, psychological, social, and cultural" (196). In the case of animals, these positive freedoms and how to respect them will be specific to the species and context. Indeed, there is no one unifying characteristic or capacity that magically bestows moral standing only on humans, or only on certain animal species. James Rachels (2004) argues that:

> There is no such thing as moral standing *simpliciter*. Rather, moral standing is always moral standing with respect to some particular mode of treatment…It is appropriate to direct moral consideration toward any individual who has any of the indefinitely long list of characteristics that constitute morally good reasons why he or she should not be treated in any of the various ways in which individuals may be treated…We would distinguish three elements: what is done to the individual; the reason for doing it or not doing it, which connects the action to some benefit or harm to the individual; and the pertinent facts about the individual that help to explain why he or she is susceptible to that particular benefit or harm. (170)

In my view, both marginal humans and animals possess autonomy in a minimal sense, as opposed to normal adult humans, who possess autonomy at a richer level. Paternalism is normally understood to be a threat to autonomous people, as it can result in coercion and can compromise the ability to make free choices. For those who are autonomous in the minimal sense, paternalism can be beneficial when applied with the goal of protecting the individual from harm by others. In this way, as Rachels (2004) pointed out, an understanding of the degree to which an individual is autonomous can meet the criteria of explaining why he or she is susceptible to harms or benefits in ways that others are not. That is, my view maintains the value of all autonomous individuals while providing a way to guide our actions towards them, whereas those who only endorse the rich view of autonomy would neglect marginal humans and animals. In the case of a child or companion animal, adult humans act as guardians to protect their interests, while at the same time acknowledging and respecting their minimal autonomy.

Kristin Andrews (2013) puts forth a similar argument in what she calls, the "umbrella view" of autonomy, which suggests that human children and teenagers should be included as moral agents, and some animals. Andrews is attempting to respond to Kantian-type arguments, like that of Christine Korsgaard's (examined in its own right in Chap. 6), whereby autonomy requires the ability to mind read or the possession of a theory of mind to decide whether an act is justified and to then act on that judgment. This ability is referred to as normative self-government, and in these kinds of arguments it is what separates humans as moral agents from other animals who can only act on the basis of their desires. Acting for rational reasons means being conscious of *what* one desires, as well as being conscious *that* one desires. Andrews summarizes this sort of argument, saying:

> A straightforward argument that moral agency requires having a theory of mind begins with the idea that moral agency requires autonomy, and autonomy requires acting for reasons, which in turn requires realizing that you have reasons for performing an action. Since reasons for action are sets of beliefs and desires that motivate behavior, and having a theory of mind is the ability to think about beliefs and desires, it follows that acting for reasons requires having a theory of mind. Or so the argument goes. (2013, p. 179).

Andrews is concerned that the consequences of such a view of autonomy are the exclusion of human children as moral agents, and potentially other "apes". She argues that it is not only the ability to consider one's own beliefs and desires that can give rise to something like normative self-government. Other cognitive capacities are also able to do this. Making reference to studies on the moral development of children, she says that although children might not be able to fully evaluate their reasons for acting, we still retain moral language and judgments when describing their behaviours. This is because children are still developing their cognitive capacities, and so they are only limited in terms of their abilities to control impulses and emotions, but they are still able to act on the basis of reasons. In this way, we can talk about the degrees of cognitive capacities that are required for normative self-government, which means that normative self-government itself also admits to degrees (Andrews 2013, p. 180).

Another reason Andrews gives to support the idea that autonomy exists in degrees is by providing ways in which the cognitive capacities of children and apes meet the criteria of autonomy as defined by John Christman (2015). According to his definition of autonomy: "to be autonomous is to be one's own person, to be directed by considerations, desires, conditions, and characteristics that are not simply imposed externally upon one, but are part of what can somehow be considered one's authentic self." (Christman 2015). And so, Andrews argues that we can identify a person who is directed by internal considerations by figuring out whether or not she can distinguish intentional from non-intentional action. If an individual can do this, then it implies that she not only recognizes intentionality in others, but also in herself. She concludes that, based on numerous studies, both human children and apes can understand intentional actions both in others and themselves. In addressing the second component of Christman's definition of autonomy, Andrews further claims that it is reasonable to assume that acting from one's authentic self means the ability to self-create. This is done, according to her, by purposefully changing oneself. Although there is very little direct evidence to support the idea that children and apes possess this ability, there have been observations made that both are able to engage in observational learning, whereby individuals can modify their own personalities (Andrews 2013, pp. 182–183).

From all of this, Andrews reaffirms her claim that understanding autonomy as an umbrella concept that admits to degrees, and that includes a variety of cognitive capacities, results in the inclusion in the moral sphere of children, unreflective human adults and, possibly, great apes. Some of these capacities might include a theory of mind, the ability to recognize intentional agency in others, and the ability to learn from others and from one's own experiences (Andrews 2013, p. 183). Indeed, as I claimed in Chap. 2, more than just apes and human children seem to possess these abilities, and so, while I agree with Andrews that autonomy consists of a variety of cognitive capacities that exist in varying degrees, I am arguing for an even more inclusive concept of autonomy that would include any animal that has a sense of self, and who can act as a result of reasons. This means that my own view of minimal autonomy requires even less complex mental capacities than Andrews requires for her own view. At any rate, her argument is valuable insofar as it challenges the concept of autonomy as normative self-government that only humans can possess. By arguing that there are other cognitive capacities that can be used to engage in self-governance and self-creation, she opens the door to the notion that autonomy exists in degrees. In addition, if we include the arguments provided in support of the agency, intentionality, and selfhood of animals to this sort of umbrella view of autonomy, it becomes clear that minimal autonomy can be understood simply as the freedom to act on the basis of one's own reasons.

Aiming for Consistency

When it comes to making ethical judgments, our broad aim is for consistency. That is, we generally believe that to be fair or just, our ethical judgments should not be based on arbitrary prejudice or emotional reactions. Instead, they should be based on rational principles or moral concepts that apply to individuals, groups, and across contexts and different situations. For humans, we typically believe that we owe others moral obligations by virtue of certain qualities they possess, such as autonomy and agency. If people possess these qualities, then we owe them moral obligations, and we do this to varying degrees depending on the complexity of the qualities as they are found in different individuals. This is why the nature and extent of our moral obligations towards others vary, as in the differences between what we owe (morally) towards other adults or towards children, or towards those who are intellectually disabled, and so on. What we agree on is the importance and value of respecting the autonomy of others, when and where we find it.

In my view, autonomy exists when an individual is understood to be an agent who acts on the basis of their own beliefs, desires, and preferences, and who is also self-aware. As many animals share these qualities with humans, as I have argued above, then we also owe them moral obligations in the form of respecting their autonomy. In this way, we are acting consistently, in terms of our moral behaviour. If we deny that we have direct moral obligations towards animals, despite the evidence that they possess agency, self-awareness (even minimally), and autonomy, just as humans do, to a greater or lesser extent, then we are simply acting inconsistently and irrationally. Sometimes this is the result of acting based on our desires and emotions. So, while moral theories based on care and compassion should not be discounted, it is important to supplement them with rational principles or guidelines, even abstract ones, to achieve greater consistency, and thereby greater justice, in our relationships with other animals. Respecting the autonomy of other individuals, both human and animal, requires both a rational recognition and an acknowledgement of the value of freedom in others, as well as the emotional motivation to act on it in caring and compassionate ways. In this way, using autonomy as the ground for moral obligations towards animals ensures a consistency in our treatment of them, regardless of whether or not we have personal relationships with those animals. For example, animals that are remote from us, such as wild or agricultural animals, will still be recognized as worthy of direct moral obligations on the ground of autonomy, even if we do not feel an emotional connection to them, like we might towards our own companion animals.

Autonomy and Duties

The link between selfhood and autonomy that I am arguing for also finds support in the work of Alan Gewirth (1978), who provides an account of autonomy that is based on fundamental features of the self.

Although we differ profoundly in our conclusions regarding the autonomous status of animals, in what follows, I explain his theory of self, agency, and autonomy and in what ways it enriches my own view.

Gewirth's argument can be summarized in a few main claims. For simplicity, these are outlined below by Evelyn Pluhar (1995):

1. "I do X for end or purpose E."
2. "E is good."
3. "My freedom and well-being are necessary goods."
4. "I must have freedom and well-being."
5. "I have rights to freedom and well-being." (Self-Fulfillment, pp. 81–82)
6. "All other persons ought at least to refrain from removing or interfering with my freedom and well-being."
7. "I have rights to freedom and well-being because I am a prospective purposive agent."
8. "If the having of some quality Q is a sufficient condition of some predicate P's belonging to some individual S, then P must also belong to all other subjects that have Q."
9. "All prospective purposive agents have rights to freedom and well-being."
10. "Act in accordance with the generic rights of your recipients as well as of yourself." (1995, pp. 243–244)

Gewirth believes that his argument must be accepted on logical grounds by every rational agent, as all purposive action is a result of an agent acting towards the achievement of what seems "good" to her. From this, he derives the supreme principle of morality stated as, "Act in accord with the generic rights of your recipients as well as of yourself" (1978, p. 135). As such, one can argue that all autonomous agents are deserving of rights, and this means respecting their autonomy in both negative and positive ways. Negatively, agents have the right to be free from direct or indirect compulsions; positively, by being in control of their own actions through freedom of choice. We are obligated to protect these positive rights in others.

It is by virtue of the selfhood of the agent that the supreme principle of morality exists at all. For Gewirth, "The self, person, or agent to whom the choices belong may be viewed as an organized system of dispositions in which such informed reasons are coherently interrelated with other desires and choices. Insofar as a person's behavior derives from this system, it is the person who controls his behavior by his unforced choice, so that it is voluntary. And because it is voluntary, it constitutes part of the justificatory basis of the supreme principle of morality." (1978, p. 31) Gewirth describes the "prospective purposive agent" as someone who simply has purposes she wants to fulfil. The mere possession of purposes is enough to grant someone rights to the freedom to attain those purposes, by his account. It is as a consequence of this that, as someone who desires to act, you must also claim those conditions that allow you to act, and thus you must claim rights to autonomy.

Gewirth considers the application of this theory to non-human animals in one page, where he argues that animals lack the potentialities for agency, and thus they do not have the generic rights humans do. He believes that animals are deserving of protection against "wanton infliction of pain" due to the similarity of feelings of pain that animals share with humans. He also argues that the freedom of animals must be subordinated to the freedom of humans when the rights of humans are infringed upon. It is interesting, however, that in an earlier part of the same book, where he is describing the importance of the agent's ability to control his own behaviour, he explains how it is we know that the ability to act freely is valued by someone as an intrinsic good: "In addition to this instrumental value, the agent also regards his freedom as intrinsically good, simply because it is an essential component of purposive action and indeed of the very possibility of action. This is shown by the fact that when he is subjected to violence, coercion, or physical constraint, he may react negatively, with dislike, annoyance, dissatisfaction, anger, hostility, outrage, or similar negative emotions, even when he has no further specific end in view." (Gewirth 1978, p. 52) Non-human animals react in the same ways when subjected to the same constraints on their behaviour. According to his own argument, if their reactions are the same, then they must also value their abilities to act freely and without constraint.

As I see it, it is by virtue of the shared capacity for agency, characteristic of self-awareness, between humans and other animals that provides the basis of autonomy for both. This does not mean that they possess the same degree of autonomy, or that they are both moral agents. For being a moral agent is not required for moral rights, even by Gewirth's (1978) account. He includes marginal agents, such as very young and mentally disabled humans, in his rights view, as they too have desires and purposes, which include food, drink, shelter, and companionship. Purposiveness is what grants these individuals full rights, even if their freedoms must be limited at times to prevent them from causing harm to themselves or others due to their limited capacity to rationally evaluate their reasons for acting in accordance with their desires. Gewirth accords rights to those with even the most minimal desires, such as newborn babies, by virtue of their purposiveness.

Why, then, does he not see that his argument must also logically apply to most non-human mammals? This is especially worrisome given that there are many cases where adult non-human mammals have more complex desires and abilities to achieve their goals than newborn babies or intellectually disabled human adults. It seems that the likeliest answer is simply due to his ignorance of the biological and ethological research into animal minds which supports their possession of self-awareness and intelligence. For if he acknowledged, even at the simplest level, that non-human animals have desires and purposes, then he must admit to their rights to freedom and autonomy to fulfil them. Given my own view on animals and selfhood, in conjunction with Gewirth's theory of autonomy, animals must be autonomous by virtue of their purposiveness. On this point we would disagree. However, I do agree with Gewirth that given this selfhood and autonomy, animals are thus deserving of rights, in the same ways humans are. We simply cannot deny these rights, based on minimal agency, as a result of speciesism or homocentrism, without being guilty of logical inconsistency. The extent to which we must sometimes restrict certain freedoms of both human and non-human animals for their own safety, would be determined in a similar fashion, as it would be based on the level of rationality and thus the ability to evaluate available options for action in light of the nature of their desires and goals. For, as we all know, sometimes the restriction of certain actions is for the greater good of the overall or longer term freedoms of an individual, even if they do not see it that way themselves. In the case of animals, we rely on the increasing body of research and knowledge regarding different species and their respective traits to guide us towards actions that would best respect their autonomy and freedoms.

A Naturalized View of Autonomy

A more naturalized account of autonomy that is grounded in the idea of an evolutionary continuity between humans and animals does not require robust notions of reflective, rational agency to establish the moral significance of animals who have a basic sense of self. One such view, as developed by Bruce Waller (1998), argues that autonomy can be understand as autonomy-as-alternatives, whereby alternative possibilities for action are a result of options provided by the natural environment around us. Rather than choices being explained by a mysterious uncaused self-willing of sorts that is independent of environmental factors, Waller argues that since animals are products of their environment, their choices are shaped by the options that are available to them. He describes autonomy-as-alternatives in this way:

> We do not want freedom for choices with no causal antecedents, freedom from all environmental contingencies, freedom to make inexplicable choices. To the contrary,…we (humans and white-footed mice) want to be able to act otherwise if we choose otherwise; that is, we want other options available when we experience different circumstances in our changing environment…The choice made is the result of complex environmental influences, including the long-term environmental history that shaped the species to occasionally explore different paths. The choice nonetheless meets the white-footed mouse autonomy requirements: not a choice independent of all natural influences, but instead one of many open alternatives that can be followed in a changing environment under "different circumstances". (Waller 1998, p. 11)

For Waller, the difference between human and animal autonomy is based on the capacity for abstract reasoning, which allows humans to identify a wider range of alternative possibilities for action presented in their environment. This is closest to the rich sense or common view of autonomy as I have presented it, and it explains why such importance has been placed on the reflective capacities of humans who are able to anticipate such things as the possible consequences of their actions, hopes for the future, goal-setting, and so on. This rich sense of autonomy correlates with a rich level of selfhood, where a person can reflect on the kind of person they are or desire to be, and direct their actions and choices in accordance with the possibilities their environment affords them to achieve their goals. This is also characteristic of autonomy understood as normative self-government, as it is posited by Kantians.

Most animals that possess the basic level of selfhood are autonomous in their actions as they are able to choose between the alternative paths provided in their environments. The more complex the level of selfhood a species or an individual has, the more alternatives they are able to recognize in their environment. Social animals, for example, exhibit more complex patterns of behaviours and wider ranges of emotions as a result of their cognitive capacities. For example, if an experiment is being performed on a dog where she is subjected to an invasive surgical procedure, and where a wound is left open for better observation, she will be restricted in her movements and she will not be allowed to play or interact with other dogs. Her physical pain is alleviated by medication. From this experiment, we can see that the dog's possibilities for action are limited and restrict the freedom she has to act socially, for example. This would most likely lead to boredom and abnormal repetitive behaviours, which are considered to be accurate indicators of emotional suffering. It is not just that she is free from physical suffering that is morally relevant, but also that her autonomy to positively fulfil her interests and preferences, as a member of a social species, have been greatly reduced by those performing the experiment. Restricting available options for animals to act by restricting their environment is one way that humans can disrespect autonomy in animals, as it limits their choices.

Some would argue that a rich level of autonomy is the only kind of autonomy worth caring about or worth respecting in others. Some would say that having one's goals in life restricted by others is worse than being locked in a cage. What is mistaken here is the assumption that we should *only* value the rich level of autonomy and not also the basic level of autonomy. We do value the basic level of autonomy in ourselves, perhaps even more so than the richer level as it gives us the luxury of increased options for action. That is, the basic options for action are needed prior to and in order for richer options to be available to us. If I am locked in a cage, or starving, or deprived of all social contact, then my basic level of autonomy has been violated, and I am unable to act on alternative possibilities in the richer sense because they are simply not available to me. Indeed, the suffering caused by restrictions on my basic needs can be far worse than restrictions placed on my richer interests. And so, we must consider further how autonomy gives rise to and affects our moral obligations to other animals, which is the subject of the next section.

Obligations Towards Animals

To respect the autonomy of animals, we would need to make some radical changes to our current treatments of them. To determine how we ought to treat animals that are already kept in captivity (in zoos, for example), we would have to begin by learning about the kind of animal self we are concerned with, and to what extent they are self-aware. For example, in the case of a captive dolphin, we would need to gather and analyze research on dolphin mentality to better understand what kinds of interests dolphins have, so that we can have a fuller account of the dolphin self. This will allow us to identify the level of autonomy dolphins have, so that we can act in ways that respect that autonomy.

For example, a utilitarian view would suggest that as long as the dolphin is free from pain, and has its needs for survival met, then there is no moral problem involved in its captivity. In my view, respecting the captive dolphin's autonomy requires such things as a variety of different natural environments, much larger containment areas, and much greater opportunities for social interaction with other dolphins than currently exist. It would also mean that its interests could not be overridden by human interests as easily as they are now. We do not believe it is right to override the autonomy of other humans for reasons that are unnecessary, such as for entertainment, or economic gain, where someone is used merely as a means to one's own end. In the case of dolphins, this would mean that it is not acceptable to capture dolphins and keep them in captivity merely as a means for our own entertainment. To do so would be to disrespect the autonomy of wild dolphins to live their lives without harmful human interference.

To study the minds of animals also raises questions of autonomy, as many experiments are performed in laboratories under unnatural conditions. Not only does this affect the results of such studies, but it can also harm the autonomy of these animals by the restrictions placed on their natural behaviours. In my view, the practices of cognitive ethology, which consist mainly of observing animal behaviour in natural settings, are preferable to experiments in laboratories since they respect animal autonomy by allowing them the freedom to act according to their own desires. If required, animals kept in captivity for experimental purposes should be provided with the most freedom possible, in terms of their living environment and behaviours. If this is not possible, then the experiments should not occur.

For domesticated animals, such as companion animals and pets, respecting their autonomy consists in allowing them to make their own choices to the greatest extent possible. This can be difficult to navigate as these animals live within human environments where such behaviours as scenting furniture or dragging in killed prey are not appreciated. However, by understanding the kinds of desires and preferences that, for example, dogs have can allow for accommodations within the home that respect their autonomy. Providing opportunities for running, socializing with other dogs, playing, and so on, demonstrates this respect, as these are the things required for well-being and good health.

Respecting autonomy in animals will mean revising their status under the law, along with much more careful thinking about what kinds of choices are available to them as a result of their mental capacities, and how we need to alter our own actions to best respect the autonomy they have to make those choices. For many, this would be difficult as beliefs about animals as objects or merely possessions is so deeply ingrained in our human culture. One can also be sceptical about the ability of humans to respect autonomy at all, given the violence and abuse towards other humans that abounds in society. However, it is a moral ideal and ethical goal to strive towards that, as I have argued, is supported by strong arguments and evidence.

Autonomy is the morally valuable feature of a self-aware creature. Autonomy would not exist if there were no capacity for phenomenal self-awareness or self-consciousness. This is because self-awareness is what allows creatures to identify with their own desires, preferences, or interests. This also means that potential options for action matter to self-aware creatures, because they allow for choice, and the freedom to choose among alternate possibilities, without restriction or constraint.

Greater levels of self-awareness create more complex beliefs, desires, and preferences, in part through rational reflection, so there will be more factors to consider when attempting to respect the autonomy of a human as opposed to that of a mouse, for example. But, in both cases, it is still correct to refer to each creature as autonomous. The preference of the mouse could simply be to follow one route to its food source rather than another, while the preference of a human could be to study philosophy rather than psychology. In both cases, actions taken to limit these options, or to force upon each creature one path rather than the alternative they desire, effectively reduce their autonomy. Not all humans share the same level of autonomy. Certainly some primates, for example, have a richer level of autonomy than severely intellectually disabled humans. But as long as there is self-awareness, even in a minimal form, autonomy still exists for these humans, as well as many animals.

Why should we care about the autonomy of the mouse at all? Simply put, it is because we value freedom, and the ability to make our own choices. Autonomy, in its most basic form, is simply the ability to have control over one's own life and actions. Possessing self-awareness involves an evaluative aspect that allows one to have an idea or sense of how one wants to live, and an awareness of one's own desires and preferences, as the grounds for making choices. As such, we generally believe that we ought to respect autonomy where and when we find it. And there doesn't seem to be any good reason why we would not extend the respect for autonomy to animals as well as humans. We believe that it is a good for an individual to pursue its own ends to the greatest extent possible. That is not to say that conflicts between autonomous individuals will not occur, or force us to choose to respect or deny autonomy for certain individuals in specific cases. But the goal should be to respect and/or increase the opportunities to exercise autonomy when possible.

It might be argued that it is too difficult a task to understand accurately what an animal desires, or how our actions might infringe on their autonomy. In part, these concerns might be due to the fear of anthropomorphism, or they may be a result of scepticism about the ability of animals to possess beliefs and concepts in the same ways that humans do, or scepticism about whether or not we can know adequately the content of animal beliefs, if they do possess them. I have attempted to address these concerns in the previous chapters, but I also want to add another type of response that relates more directly to how we might respect the autonomy of animals in practice. Consent, or more specifically, informed consent, is an important consideration when we are attempting to respect the autonomy of human beings. If someone did not consent to a particular form of treatment by another, then we believe that person's autonomy has been violated. Humans can give consent in various ways, and in various forms, both verbally and through written communication. However, with animals the situation is clearly different. Animals are unable to vocalize or withhold their consent. Andrew Linzey (2009) notes this problem and argues that although animals can show behavioural indications of consent, or a lack thereof, it is a presumption on our part rather than a voluntary, verbal form of consent, like that which takes place between humans. What this means is that we ought to show much greater care and consideration in our relations with animals, as although I am arguing that they are autonomous, they themselves are limited in how they can express their desires and preferences to us, and they are limited by the very nature of our domestic relationships with animals in exerting control over their own actions. By viewing animals as autonomous, it places greater responsibility on humans both to attempt to interpret behavioural indications of consent (or the lack thereof), and to adjust their actions accordingly. Many animals live in some form of a domestic relationship with humans, and they will have less autonomy in general than those animals that live in the wild. But it is not difficult to see that even within these domestic relationships, animals could be accorded much more respect for their autonomy. Indeed, Linzey (2005) argues elsewhere that all we really need to know about animals to act ethically towards them is based on what we can reasonably know about what sorts of things can cause them harm. He writes:

But we do not need to know precisely how a bat thinks or feels or mentally encounters the world in order to know basic things about how it can be harmed, for example, by mutilation, by deprivation of its instincts, by isolation from its peers, by subjecting it to invasive procedures and by the infliction of adverse physical stimuli. We can, and do, know these things without scientific evidence and without knowing everything possible, philosophically or scientifically, about the mental consciousness of a bat. We can know these things, at least, *as reasonably* as we know them in the case of most humans. (2005, p. 72).

This applies to the idea of respecting autonomy, and not just to knowing how to avoid harming animals in general, although avoiding causing harm to animals is certainly one way to show respect for their autonomy. We can reasonably know that an animal would not consent to being isolated from its peers, or to an invasive or painful procedure. But we can also reasonably claim to know that an animal desires freedom of choice to pursue its own interests in a positive way, to the greatest extent possible without human interference. This means that even within domestic relationships with animals, humans can limit their interference in the choices those animals make as much as possible. We tend to picture this as taking the form of letting animals run free, which obviously would not benefit them in terms of their health and safety. Letting the dogs I live with run out of the front door would most certainly mean injury or death when they attempt to cross the highway to get to the park beyond. Instead, knowing that they desire to run in the park, I respect that desire by taking them there safely. Disrespecting the autonomy of a companion dog might take the form of chaining it to a tree and never respecting its desire for affection or exercise. This might all sound like simple common sense, but by emphasizing that these actions are a result of the autonomous nature of animals, it allows us to evaluate our interactions with them and improve on them by recognizing the value we place on freedom of choice, in both humans and animals. Just as we can determine how to treat other humans based on a notion of how to respect their autonomy to the greatest extent possible, so too can we reasonably assess the best ways to respect the autonomy of the animals we interact with. Accepting the notion that autonomy can exist in both minimal and rich forms, depending on the individual animal and their capacities for agency and self-awareness, gives us a guide as to how we ought to treat other animals in specific ways as it challenges us to not only identify the things that harm them, but also those things that benefit them.

Conclusion

Autonomy can be defined in many ways, and I have provided an outline in this chapter of what I call the common view of autonomy, which posits that only humans can be autonomous beings by virtue of their ability to reflect rationally on their choices and guide their own lives. I have challenged this common view, based on the idea that animals who are self-aware agents, to a greater or lesser degree, can also be considered autonomous in minimal and rich ways. Animals that are minimally autonomous are still able to act as a result of their own reasons, and the freedom to do so is what we respect in others, and the grounds for directing moral obligations towards them. I have also argued that by accepting a minimal notion of autonomy we are obligated to respect it in those animals who possess it, and that this view provides a guide to making decisions about our interactions with those animals. In the next chapter I consider other views of animal ethics that both complement my own and challenge the notion that what we ought to respect first and foremost in our relationships with other animals is autonomy.

References

Andrews, K. (2013). Ape autonomy? Social norms and moral agency in other species. In K. Petrus & M. Wild (Eds.), *Animal minds & animal ethics: Connecting two separate fields* (pp. 173–195). Bielefeld: transcript Verlag.

Arpaly, N. (2003). *Unprincipled virtue: An inquiry into moral agency*. Toronto: Oxford University Press.

Christman, J. (2015). Autonomy in moral and political philosophy. In E. N. Zalta (Ed.), *The Stanford encyclopedia of philosophy* (Spring ed.). Retrieved from http://plato.stanford.edu/archives/spr2015/entries/autonomy-moral

Dworkin, G. (1988). *The theory and practice of autonomy*. New York: Cambridge University Press.

Frey, R. G. (1987). Autonomy and the value of animal life. *The Monist, 70*, 50–63.

Gewirth, A. (1978). *Reason and morality*. Chicago: The University of Chicago Press.

Linzey, A. (2005). What prevents us from recognizing animal sentience? In J. Turner & J. D'Silva (Eds.), (2006). *Animals, ethics and trade: The challenge of animal sentience* (pp. 68–78). Sterling: Earthscan.

Linzey, A. (2009). *Why animal suffering matters: Philosophy, theology, and practical ethics*. Toronto: Oxford University Press.

Pluhar, E. B. (1995). *Beyond prejudice: The moral significance of human and nonhuman animals*. Durham: Duke University Press.

Rachels, J. (2004). Drawing lines. In C. R. Sunstein & M. C. Nussbaum (Eds.), *Animal rights: Current debates and new directions* (pp. 162–174). Toronto: Oxford University Press.

Rachels, J., & Ruddick, W. (1989). Lives and liberty. In J. Christman (Ed.), *The inner citadel: Essays on individual autonomy* (pp. 221–233). New York: Oxford University Press.

Regan, T. (1983). *The case for animal rights*. Berkeley: University of California Press.

Richards, D. A. J. (1989). Rights and autonomy. In J. Christman (Ed.), *The inner citadel: Essays on individual autonomy* (pp. 203–220). New York: Oxford University Press.

Rogers, L., & Kaplan, G. (2004). All animals are not equal: The interface between scientific knowledge and legislation for animal rights. In C. R. Sunstein & M. C. Nussbaum (Eds.), *Animal rights: Current debates and new directions* (pp. 175–204). Toronto: Oxford University Press.

Rowlands, M. (2012). *Can animals be moral?* Toronto: Oxford University Press.

Waller, B. N. (1998). *The natural selection of autonomy*. New York: State University of New York Press.

Wise, S. M. (2002). *Drawing the line: Science and the case for animal rights*. Cambridge: Perseus Books.

5

Other Views of Animal Ethics

Introduction

In the previous three chapters I argued that what makes an animal morally considerable is the capacity for agency and selfhood, and that the degree to which an animal is self-aware indicates the corresponding degree of autonomy that we ought to respect with regard to our treatment of them. My approach is not dissimilar to other philosophers who take a *capacity orientation* to the study of animal ethics. This is because, when we try to understand the reasons for taking anyone, human or animal, as morally important, it is difficult to determine just what underlies our moral obligations. I believe it is of the utmost importance to question the reasons why we care for others, and so, instead of taking a relational or caring perspective in ethics I prefer to dig deeper into just what it is to be a creature worthy of care and consideration. Once this has been established, it can lead to more accurate views on how we ought to care for others, both human and animal, and the resulting relationships we have with each other. So, regardless of which moral theory you prefer, it will inevitably conclude that it is their capacities that distinguish the moral significance of, and differences between, rocks and dogs, or dolphins and humans.

Just as I have argued that agency, self-awareness, and autonomy are the most morally relevant features of individuals, other philosophers have focused on certain capacities shared by humans and other animals. However, in this chapter I argue that my own account more thoroughly and accurately addresses why animals are morally considerable and to what extent we owe individuals from different species fewer or greater moral obligations. Specifically, I examine one utilitarian view and two rights views that are dominant in the study of animal ethics, along with an alternative view that is based on a relational and caring perspective. I believe that these views are best represented by the arguments of Peter Singer, Tom Regan, Bernard Rollin, and Lori Gruen, respectively.

As well as providing a general summary of each of these philosopher's arguments in favour of the moral consideration of animals, I focus on a few particular questions, including: What capacity makes animals morally considerable? To what extent do we owe animals moral consideration based on this capacity? Should we focus on mental capacities as the grounds for the moral consideration of animals at all? I examine what kinds of conceptual and practical problems result from each view and how these problems can be better addressed by including a consideration of agency, self-awareness, and autonomy.

Peter Singer and Utilitarianism

Peter Singer's (1993) theory of animal ethics is an extension of the principle of the equal consideration of interests, to non-human animals, particularly as it is found in utilitarianism. This principle requires us to take into consideration the interests of all those affected by our actions, regardless of our own personal characteristics or those of others, when we make ethical judgments. Equality is an important feature of Singer's view of utilitarianism, and this principle provides an objective method of weighing everyone's interests without personal bias.

Singer is a preference utilitarian, which means that an individual's preferences, in the form of interests, should be considered by others when

5 Other Views of Animal Ethics

making moral decisions. According to this theory, we ought to weigh the interests of all those involved, and determine who stands to be harmed or benefited by the action in question, so that our action will bring about the least amount of suffering and greatest amount of pleasure for all those affected. In order to treat everyone equally, we ought to consider the interests of all those affected without prejudice; there is no good reason, according to Singer, to place more value or weight on the interests of one person over another. This is the importance of the principle of equal consideration of interests. It allows for a non-biased evaluation of interests that is not dependent on such features as race, religion, gender, or in this case, species. Singer writes:

> The essence of the principle of equal consideration of interests is that we give equal weight in our moral deliberations to the like interests of all those affected by our actions. This means that if only X and Y would be affected by a possible act, and if X stands to lose more than Y stands to gain, it is better not to do the act…What the principle really amounts to is this: an interest is an interest, whoever's interest it may be. (1993, p. 21)

The last line in this extract is most important in the application of this principle to animals, because it means that the only interests that matter are those based on the capacity to suffer or experience pleasure. These interests are not determined by race, gender, or species, as the capacity to suffer is not dependent on these traits. That is not to say that the causes of suffering are not related to these traits, as we know that racism, sexism, or speciesism can cause suffering specific to those who possess them. It simply means that the capacity to suffer and to experience pleasure is a feature shared by most animals, both human and non-human, and that they are interests worthy of moral consideration. Whether animals have interests beyond these are a matter of debate and, for Singer, are dependent on the characteristics of specific species.

When Singer applies the principle of equal consideration of interests to animals, he begins by quoting a passage by Jeremy Bentham that foresees the application of utilitarianism to animals as well as humans. This passage is worth quoting, as it provides such a clear explanation of the significance of sentience for moral consideration. Bentham wrote:

The day may come when the rest of the animal creation may acquire those rights which never could have been withholden from them but by the hand of tyranny. The French have already discovered that the blackness of the skin is no reason why a human being should be abandoned without redress to the caprice of a tormentor. It may one day come to be recognized that the number of the legs, the villosity of the skin, or the termination of the *os sacrum*, are reasons equally insufficient for abandoning a sensitive being to the same fate. What else is it that should trace the insuperable line? Is it the faculty of reason, or perhaps the faculty of discourse? But a fullgrown horse or dog is beyond comparison a more rational, as well as a more conversable animal, than an infant of a day, or a week, or even a month, old. But suppose they were otherwise, what would it avail? The question is not, Can they *reason*? Nor Can they *talk*? but, *Can they suffer*? (Singer 1993, p. 57)

Here, Bentham argues that just as skin colour has been rejected as a barrier to moral consideration based on suffering, so too will species membership be rejected as a barrier to moral consideration based on suffering, as any being capable of feeling is also capable of being tormented by those with more power. This capacity for sentience becomes the foundation for Singer's more developed argument that animals are morally equal to humans in terms of the consideration of their interests for suffering and enjoyment. Sentience is the basis for all moral consideration, for Singer, as it is the necessary condition for the possession of interests at all. Indeed, Singer argues that "The capacity for suffering and enjoying things is a prerequisite for having interests at all, a condition that must be satisfied before we can speak of interests in any meaningful way…If a being suffers, there can be no moral justification for refusing to take that suffering into consideration." (1993, p. 57)

Because sentience underlies all other interests, and the weighing of interests is the basis of utilitarian decision-making, sentience is "the only defensible boundary of concern for the interests of others" (Singer 1993, p. 58). As many non-human animals are sentient, the principle of equal consideration of interests applies to them in the same way it applies to all humans. Indeed, those who refuse to consider animals under this principle of equality for no other reason than giving preference to the interests of members of their own species are referred to as speciesists by Singer, which denotes its similarity to racism and sexism. This simply means that when we give weight to the interests of certain sentient beings based on traits that are irrelevant to the capacity to suffer, we are acting in an unjustifiably biased way. In the case of animals, the belief that humans are more intelligent or more spiritually valuable than non-human animals and therefore have the right to treat animals without any moral consideration is wrong and speciesist. This is because it denies the moral importance of suffering and enjoyment as the basis of all other interests for both humans and animals.

Significantly, the principle of equal consideration of interests does not necessarily result in equal treatment, and in each case the amount of suffering of all those involved would need to be measured and compared to conclude who is suffering most. Priority must be given to whoever is suffering most under the circumstances, whether human or non-human animal. Although the capacity to suffer itself is not usually the *most* concerning issue or problem under this theory, the amount of suffering may be affected by other capacities that differ between species. Singer (1993) argues "that we must take care when we compare the interests of different species" (58) and that, "there are many areas in which the superior mental powers of normal adult humans make a difference: anticipation, more detailed memory, greater knowledge of what is happening, and so on…it is the mental anguish that makes the human's position so much harder to bear" (60). The complexity of various cognitive capacities increases one's ability to suffer mentally and emotionally in ways that other humans with diminished mental capacities may not, or that other species may not possess at all, or may possess but to a lesser degree. The less complex the mental capacities someone has, the less they can suffer, seems to be the point here. Although Singer states that in some cases animals may suffer more than humans because of their limited capacity to understand the situation they are in, he clearly believes that only humans can suffer from mental anguish in addition to physical forms of suffering. His response to the concern that it is impossible to know and compare the suffering of different species is that "precision is not essential", so long as the total quantity of suffering is reduced in the universe by treating animals in ways that would reduce or eliminate their suffering, even if the interests of humans are not affected at all (Singer 1993, p. 61).

Singer's arguments have had an undeniable impact on the moral status of animals in society, and he has successfully argued that the capacity to suffer is what makes animals morally considerable, and that this trait is shared with humans. He believes that, on the whole, we ought to reduce the use of animals in experiments that cause suffering and that, broadly speaking, we should adopt a vegetarian diet if, by doing so, it does not result in suffering and harms to us. However, Singer's view does not go far enough in terms of the full range of moral obligations we owe animals by virtue of their interests, agency, and selfhood. I believe that this weakness relates to the omission of personhood and autonomy from his theory, and that the problems that arise as a result of the aggregation of interests that occur in all forms of utilitarian calculus are due to the denial of animal selfhood and autonomy.

Although Singer advocates for the cessation of eating animals on the grounds that current factory farming methods create an overall increase in aggregate suffering in the world, he admits that the *replaceability argument* justifies the killing of animals under certain conditions. For example, if chickens are killed painlessly and replaced by other chickens who would otherwise not have existed, who themselves go on to live pleasurable lives, then there is nothing wrong with killing chickens (1993, pp. 133–134). This justification of killing comes from his view of persons and non-persons. For Singer:

> A self-conscious being is aware of itself as a distinct entity, with a past and a future…A being aware of itself in this way will be capable of having desires about its own future. For example, a professor of philosophy may hope to write a book demonstrating the objective nature of ethics; a student may look forward to graduating; a child may want to go for a ride in an aeroplane. To take the lives of any of these people without their consent, is to thwart their desires for the future. Killing a snail or a day-old infant does not thwart any desires of this kind, because snails and newborn infants are incapable of having such desires. (1993, p. 90)

As the principle of the equal consideration of interests specifies that we weigh like interests equally, those with more interests, due to capacities like valuing the future, will easily outweigh those who do not even have a concept of the future. To dismiss the idea that animals do not have desires for the future seems to assume that there is only one way to conceive of the future, as something that is distant from us. As we examined in Chap. 3, animals may not be able to conceive of the future specifically, but they certainly have desires for a continued existence. So, when we apply this view to animals, it means that the majority of animals are not considered to be persons by Singer, and thus it is not nearly as morally wrong to kill an animal as it is to kill a human, in the majority of relevant cases. Ultimately, Singer's argument does not entail that we stop eating animals, even under current farming practices, as the benefits for humans (including financial ones), gustatory pleasures and acting primarily in the interests of human "persons", will almost always outweigh acting in the interests of other animals (see Rowlands 2009, for further discussion on the problems with Singer's arguments regarding vegetarianism from a utilitarian perspective).

Another problem with Singer's argument concerns the omission of autonomy as the grounds for moral consideration. Consider the following example. If we were to include both human and non-human animals in an experiment, controlling all possible pain or forms of suffering for both, and the results were of great benefit to a larger populace, then we would have to ask whether anything wrong or immoral is happening. Singer would argue that as long as suffering is reduced, and greater happiness is created, then there is nothing morally wrong. However, if we recognize that the humans involved in the experiment are able to provide informed consent to be subjects in the experiment, but the non-human animals are not, there seems to be a problem. This problem, I believe, can only be explained fully by introducing the notion of autonomy.

When we ask for informed consent, we are doing so to respect the autonomy someone has in terms of freedom of choice over his or her own choices. We believe that a person should not be forced or manipulated by deception into making a decision because of their right to freedom, both positive and negative. If someone is aware of all the risks of an experiment, and chooses freely to consent to participate in the experiment then we accept that their decision is autonomous, and thus morally acceptable. In the case of non-human animals, however, they cannot consent to participate in the experiment, because they cannot understand the risks or benefits involved. Also, they cannot provide written or verbal consent, and cannot display their lack of consent at the outset, through their behaviours. Many would argue that because non-human animals cannot do this, they are not autonomous. Therefore, we only need to concern ourselves with their suffering, and as long as we control or eliminate any suffering, there is no moral harm being committed.

Autonomy, for Singer, only properly belongs to persons who are self-aware, rational, and who possess the ability to imagine a future. He not only denies that most animals possess these traits, but he also argues that autonomy is not valuable in itself, but only as one of many other interests. For example, Singer states: "Utilitarians do not respect autonomy for its own sake, although they might give great weight to a person's desire to go on living, either in a preference utilitarian way, or as evidence that the person's life was on the whole a happy one." (1993, p. 99) He believes that autonomy is a useful concept that we can choose to respect if we wish to, as it generally leads to good consequences overall for people when respected. But, because in his view, we only need to consider like interests equally, the human and non-human animal in the experiment differ because the interest of autonomy only applies to the human, as the animal is not likely to be a "person". Singer's view, while it advocates for the reduction of suffering, does not provide grounds for respecting the interests of well-being or flourishing that non-human animals have, *other than* increasing overall pleasure and reducing suffering for the aggregate whole. This problem is, in part, due to the concept of an interest it uses. As various philosophers have defined interests differently, and there is no clear consensus on what counts as an interest for humans or animals, it makes it fairly easy to define interests with a pre-determined conclusion in mind, which excludes animals from moral consideration (see, for example, Frey 1980).

One reason for Singer's denial of autonomy to animals is a result of his conception of what autonomy actually is. He states that autonomy is the ability to choose between and act upon one's own decisions and says, "Rational and self-conscious beings presumably have this ability, whereas beings who cannot consider the alternatives open to them are not capable of choosing in the required sense and hence cannot be autonomous." (1993, p. 99) He believes that while non-human animals are conscious, the majority of them are not self-conscious or rational, and so only their ability to experience pleasure and pain are morally relevant. While this view of autonomy is shared among many, there are more naturalized accounts that include both human and non-human animals, as I have argued in Chap. 4 and which I further support in Chap. 6 through an analysis of a Kantian view of autonomy. Also, there are good reasons and evidence to support the notion that animals are minimally rational and self-aware, which means that autonomy exists at more minimal levels, as well as at the more complex ones suggested here. If autonomy exists in degrees, then Singer's claims do not carry much weight.

Finally, any version of utilitarianism is subject to criticism based on the methods used to obtain the morally right answer to an ethical dilemma. Utilitarian calculus, regardless of the specific units of measurement, can often favour the interests of the many, or the whole, to the detriment of the few, or the one. One example of this kind of objection is provided by Paola Cavalieri (2001), who writes:

> According to utilitarianism, the aim of moral action is to bring about, or make likely, the best total balance of good over bad consequences—of pleasure over pain according to classical utilitarianism, of satisfaction over frustration of preferences according to the contemporary version for which Singer himself in the end opted. A fundamental objection to this all-inclusive calculation is that it doesn't sufficiently take into account the *separateness* of individuals. (91)

For humans, this results in the possibility that severely disabled infants, for example, could be experimented on if the benefits for the common good outweigh the suffering of the infants. Singer has been criticized for these sorts of implications that result from his own argument, and he has responded by saying that all this shows is that his view is truly anti-speciesist. For animals, it means that if the satisfaction of preferences for humans to eat or experiment on animals outweighs the suffering of the animals, then it is morally acceptable to do so. This is not to say Singer endorses cruelty to animals, but rather that he is unable to provide reasons that are directly based on his own arguments to counter these problems. The logical implications of Singer's view, according to Julian H. Franklin (2005), are that:

> Rodeos give much pleasure to a great number of people, so that the aggregate of pleasure for the humans is surely greater than the total of pain caused to relatively few animals. Much the same reasoning would remove

the usual objection to zoos. And for all of his misgivings, Singer has to admit, however reluctantly, that experimentation on animals cannot be excluded altogether. (11)

In my account, respect for autonomy means that individuals and minority groups cannot have their interests overridden simply for the greater good. Cases where we might override someone's autonomy would include harm to themselves or potential harm to others, and this would only occur under very serious and exceptional circumstances. Examples of this could include treating an animal medically, even if it means reducing their autonomy for a period of time, or in the case of humans, when someone threatens another with violence we reduce their autonomy by restraining them to protect the potential victim. In such cases, we normally accept an infringement of autonomy as being morally justifiable for the sake of protecting another's autonomy. I believe the best way to support this view is to adopt Kant's second formulation of the Categorical Imperative (which I argue for in Chap. 6), whereby individuals must not be treated merely as a means to someone else's ends. This means, in effect, that there are ways to respect an individual's autonomy while also gaining benefits from certain kinds of interactions. We do not have to sacrifice one for the other, but in this utilitarian theory, there is no protection against such use, and Singer's view does not provide an adequate foundation for direct moral obligations towards animals, or for individuals more broadly.

Tom Regan, Inherent Value, and Rights

Tom Regan (1983) rejects the utilitarian view of animals due to his concern that it does not account for the value an individual has regardless of their interests. For Regan, inherent value means that individuals have value in themselves, and that they are not reducible to the value attached to their experiences, preferences, or interests. Regan (1983) argues that, "They have value in their own right, a value that is distinct from, not reducible to, and incommensurate with the values of those experiences which, as receptacles, they have or undergo." (236). He compares this view of inherent value to that of utilitarian value through the use of a cup analogy:

> On the receptacle view of value, it is *what goes into the cup* (the pleasures or preference-satisfactions, for example) that has value; what does not have value is the cup itself (i.e., the individual himself or herself). The postulate of inherent value offers an alternative. The cup (that is, the individual) has value *and* a kind that is not reducible to, and is incommensurate with, what goes into the cup (e.g., pleasures), but the value of the cup (individual) is not the same as any one or any sum of the valuable things the cup contains. (Regan 1983, p. 236)

Inherent value, according to Regan, is a feature of all individuals who are a *subject of a life*, including humans and mammals over the age of one year. He specifies this because he believes that it is not simply by virtue of being conscious or alive (like plants) that something has inherent value. Instead, subjects-of-a-life are characterized by certain features, namely:

> beliefs and desires; perception, memory, and a sense of the future, including their own future; an emotional life together with feelings of pleasure and pain; preference and welfare interests; the ability to initiate action in pursuit of their desires and goals; a psychosocial identity over time; and an individual welfare in the sense that their experiential life fares well or ill for them, logically independently of their utility for others and logically independently of their being the object of anyone else's interests. (Regan 1983, p. 243)

These characteristics support the view that adult mammals, according to Regan, are intentional agents and self-conscious. He believes this to be true because when we observe and analyze the behaviours of animals it is reasonable to interpret them as intentional, and intentional behaviours are only possible if a creature is self-conscious. In more recent writings, Regan (2004) includes birds in his experiencing-subject-of-a-life category. He also discusses the possibility that fish should be considered as having rights. However, he admits that his goal is to argue for the "least controversial" cases, and that "drawing the line" as to which creatures should be included as rights-bearers is difficult beyond mammals and birds (See Regan 2004). When we attempt to draw a line between those animals that are not self-conscious and those who are, we are faced with a difficulty. But, according to Regan, we should focus on whether or not we have good reason to believe that "mammalian animals not only are conscious and sentient but also have beliefs, desires, memory, a sense of the future, self-awareness, and an emotional life, and can act intentionally" (1983, p. 77). He concludes that we do have such evidence, for reasons similar to those I explained in Chaps. 2 and 3 in the discussion on evidence of self-awareness and agency in animals.

For Regan then, the problem with utilitarianism is that it only values individuals insofar as respecting their interests increases the overall utility for all involved. The individuals themselves are not valuable for themselves, but only as "receptacles" of interests that can be judged good or bad in terms of the suffering or pleasure they bring about. Regan believes that, depending on the relevant features described above, "One either is a subject of a life, in the sense explained, or one is not. All those who are, are so equally. The subject-of-a-life criterion thus demarcates a categorical status shared by all moral agents and those moral patients with whom we are concerned." (1983, p. 245). If something or someone does not have these features, then we do not owe them direct moral obligations (like a blade of grass or a rock). If someone is a subject of a life, then they are deserving of respect and moral treatment, regardless of whether or not they are a moral agent or a moral patient. All subjects of a life are equally valuable, according to Regan, and that is why animals are deserving of rights equal to humans.

Indeed, Regan calls for the complete abolition of the use of animals in science, agriculture, and hunting in all its forms. He believes that animals should not be used for human purposes whatsoever, for any sort of human benefit, because the use of animals presupposes that animals are simply resources, with no value of their own. If they are indeed individuals with inherent value, then they are equal in value to human individuals (1983, p. 244), and this precludes their use by humans as resources of any kind.

Regan (1983) also believes that some animals are autonomous, and he distinguishes between two views of autonomy: the Kantian view; and what Regan calls preference autonomy. On the Kantian view, Regan argues that autonomy means being able to act on reasons that one can will everyone else to act on in similar circumstances, assuming that everyone's reasons would be the same as my own, arrived at through deliberation and reflection. To act on the basis of one's own deliberations is to act autonomously. This level of reasoning, according to Regan, is most likely to only belong to humans, who can reflect impartially on their own situations and those of others. He asserts that "individuals are autonomous if they have preferences and have the ability to initiate action with a view to satisfying them" (1983, pp. 84–85). He calls this view preference autonomy, and believes that it does not require one to be able to reason abstractly about the reasons for acting. Instead, according to Regan, "it is enough that one have the ability to initiate action because one has those desires or goals one has and believes, rightly or wrongly, that one's desires or purposes will be satisfied or achieved by acting in a certain way" (1983, p. 85). Regan believes that mammals, while not autonomous in the Kantian sense, are autonomous under the preference view, and that they possess the requisite cognitive capacities to act according to their own preferences. Regan defends this view against the idea that the Kantian sense of autonomy is the only true sense of autonomy by arguing that Kantian autonomy is only required in order to be a moral agent, rather than a requirement for autonomy in any sense.

To respect the autonomy of animals, we must respect their interests, in similar ways to other humans. Specifically, Regan argues that animals "live well relative to the degree to which (1) they pursue and obtain what they prefer, (2) they take satisfaction in pursuing and getting what they prefer, and (3) what they pursue and obtain is in their interests" (1983, pp. 85–86). Regan believes we ought to resist too much paternalism in order to respect the autonomy of individuals to have control over and satisfaction with the unfolding of their lives. He describes the case of a captive wolf whose desire for food is met by being fed by his keeper, but who would be more satisfied through the effort and exertion required to acquire his own food. Human and non-human animals who are prevented from acting autonomously are less satisfied and less likely to live a "good" life, and thus we must respect the liberty of both to pursue what they prefer, assuming that what they prefer is, in fact, good for them.

Regan offers more support for direct moral obligations towards animals than Singer does, by focusing on the value of the individual as something that is beyond the sum of its interests. There are, however, two main conceptual problems with his subject-of-a-life criterion and his view of autonomy that are better addressed with my own view. Also, Regan believes that the implications of his own arguments necessitate an abolitionist view on the use of animals, which I believe is somewhat misguided and can be detrimental to our understanding of the relationships we have with other animals.

An individual that is an experiencing being the subject of a life, for Regan, must possess the full list of criteria as described above to qualify as inherently valuable and deserving of rights. There are two problems with this criterion. First, some have claimed that the specific features that make up this criterion are chosen to include non-human animals and marginal humans. As Robert Garner (2005a, b) suggests, "But isn't this the wrong way round? In other words, should we not be establishing what characteristics are essential for moral considerability before describing who meets the criteria we have established? Regan points out that his subject-of-a-life principle explains the moral sameness and moral equality between humans and animals. But isn't it this very moral equality that needs explaining in the first place?" (55). This is an important consideration as any theory of animal ethics has implications for marginal cases, such as young children or people with intellectual disabilities, who are often discounted from moral consideration due to their lack of personhood in the fullest sense. To first determine what makes someone morally considerable at all and then examine whether or not animals and marginal humans possess this quality only strengthens the resulting arguments and implications for acting morally.

Evelyn Pluhar (1995) similarly points out that Regan's view that all subjects of a life are owed equal consideration and respect lies on an initial assumption that marginal humans are owed respect, but that he does not actually provide an argument to support this reflective intuition (239, 240). Adding to this, Julian H. Franklin (2005) also notes that Regan also begins with "the prereflective intuition that animals cannot be treated in just any way at all and then moves on to the idea of inherent value and the respect principle" (28). Once again, Regan's starting point has not been justified, which makes the subject-of-a-life criterion seem somewhat arbitrary.

As I have argued, minimal selfhood, agency, and autonomy are the criteria for inclusion in the moral community, regardless of species membership. This claim resulted from an investigation into what makes anyone morally considerable, rather than beginning with the assumption that marginal humans and animals are already deserving of moral treatment. This is partly a result of my previous work in environmental ethics, where the question of how non-sentient objects, such as nature or trees, can have moral standing can lead one into some absurd arguments and conclusions. Regan acknowledges this problem saying: "As in the case of nonconscious natural objects or collections of such objects, however, it must be said that it is radically unclear how the attribution of inherent value to these individuals can be made intelligible and non-arbitrary." (1983, p. 246). But this does not mean that we automatically owe animals moral obligations either, as for centuries humans have included animals within the realm of nature, and therefore outside the realm of moral consideration. My argument, based on the notion that minimal selfhood is the basis for moral consideration, allows us to investigate who possesses this quality, and thus who should rightfully be included in the moral community. Further to that, it provides us with guidance in determining the extent to which we owe an individual respect and moral consideration, which leads us to a second, and related, problem with Regan's subject-of-a-life criterion.

Another problem with Regan's argument is that the full range of mental features he includes in his criterion for a subject of a life is an all or nothing category, and it sets the bar very high for qualifying someone as having inherent value. This would make it difficult for some marginal humans and many animal species to be deserving of moral consideration and rights. Regan does anticipate this objection, and responds with the claim that his criterion is a sufficient, but not a necessary condition for attributing inherent value to individuals. It is possible, he claims, that comatose humans or sentient animals may not possess all of the conditions of a subject of a life, but may still be said to have inherent value. He argues, "Since the claim is made only that meeting this criterion is a sufficient condition of making the attribution of inherent value intelligible and nonarbitrary, it remains possible that animals that are conscious but not capable of acting intentionally, or, say, permanently comatose human beings might nonetheless be viewed as having inherent value." (1983, p. 246). The focus here, for Regan, is on the idea that his criterion provides an intelligible and non-arbitrary standard for attributing inherent value to both marginal humans and animals as moral patients, thereby including them in the category of moral considerability along with moral agents. The problem is that it is not clear why he does not simply argue that all sentient creatures, human or animal, are deserving of rights. It is not at all apparent how a comatose human, who does not exhibit any of the features of his criterion could be said to have "a life that fares well or ill for them, logically independently of their utility for us or of our taking an interest in them" (1983, p. 244). Also, it does not assist us in determining whether or not any animals, aside from adult mammals or birds, should be owed moral consideration with any real sort of clarity.

In Regan's view, anyone who fulfils his criterion for moral consideration is owed the same level of respect, and has equal rights to everyone else. In my view, an individual is owed moral consideration to the extent that they are conscious and self-aware, which makes it more plausible when considering the differences in moral obligations we owe to a fully conscious person as opposed to one who is comatose. For surely we would want to argue that we owe a fully conscious person different kinds of consideration than a comatose one, as the ways that we can respect their autonomy will be distinctively different based on their situations. That is not to say that I have not created a category for those who deserve moral consideration in a similar way to Regan, in that anyone who is conscious and minimally self-aware is morally relevant, and anything outside that category is not morally relevant at all. But, my view provides a more nuanced approach to dealing with the degrees of mental capacities that exist among humans and between species. It maintains a clear line between objects (such as plants or rocks) and subjects (such as humans and animals) and allows for the inclusion of minimally self-aware animals to be given moral consideration. Based on the extent to which a creature is self-aware, conscious, and able to act as an agent, we adjust the extent to which, and the ways in which we respect their autonomy. I believe this view avoids the problems Regan encounters when trying to justify our obligations towards marginal humans and animals.

Finally, the abolitionist stance that Regan believes is a consequence of his rights view is problematic as it creates a false dichotomy between animal welfarist and animal rights views. He argues that if we accept the view that to treat all subjects of a life equally, then we are committed to an animal rights position that entails that any use of animals for human interests must be abolished. He claims that:

> In my view, since the utilization of nonhuman animals for purposes of, among other things, fashion, research, entertainment, or gustatory delight harms them and treats as (our) resources, and since such treatment violates their right to be treated with respect, it follows that such utilization is morally wrong and ought to end. Merely to reform such institutional injustice (by resolving to eat only "happy" cows or to insist on larger cages, for example) is not enough. Morally considered, abolition is required. (Regan 2001, p. 43)

Abolitionist views go further than insisting on the cessation of animals being used in agriculture or entertainment by calling for the cessation of any use of animals at all by humans, including keeping animals as companions or interfering with wildlife. Animal welfarist views argue for the improvement of the lives of animals used by humans, such as better living conditions on farms and in research facilities. So, in Regan's view, we are left with either accepting the use of animals by humans, which disrespects their rights, or not using animals at all or in any way. Gary Francione (2008) also advocates for the complete abolition of the use of animals by humans. He believes that we should not breed animals for any reason, and that we should leave wildlife alone. Again, this is an unattainable goal as conflicts between humans and animals cannot be prevented when sharing the same planet and resources. They can, however, be reduced or approached differently by taking the agency and autonomy of animals seriously. Relationships between humans, and humans and animals, can be guided by Kant's maxim to never use anyone as purely a means to one's own end, as I explain further in Chap. 6.

I believe that we can reshape and revise the nature of our interactions with other animals, as there are many mutually beneficial relationships between humans and other animals, whereby animals are not treated merely as a means to fulfil the interests of humans. Animal-assisted therapy is one such example, where both the animal and human can benefit from their relationships and interactions with each other. Using sled dogs for transportation in northern climates is another. This is not to say that these relationships are never abusive towards the animals, but that if they are based on the kind of respect for autonomy I have presented in Chap. 4, then the relationship can be a morally good one for both the dogs and the humans who use them. The point is that there are many ways that we do interact with animals, and that we need moral principles to guide us in those interactions. To argue that we must accept complete abolition on the use of animals or else fall into utterly abusive relationships with them is an inaccurate understanding of some of our relationships with other animals. In Kantian terms, as long as the other creature is treated as an end and not simply as someone's means to their own end, then their autonomy can still be respected within a relationship where the use of one by the other is beneficial and respectful. In my view, as in Regan's, using animals purely as a means to satisfy our gustatory desires or to benefit from research on them is clearly unacceptable, as are most of the current relationships we have with animals for other selfish reasons.

Regan provides a much stronger argument in support of the direct moral consideration towards animals than Singer does, and my view coincides with his regarding the importance and moral value of experiencing subjects. However, I believe that my own view provides a more nuanced account of the extent to which we owe individuals moral consideration than Regan's, and that it results in better applications which more directly support the idea that further research into animal minds is important to attain a more widespread acceptance of animals as autonomous selves. As my own view is not an abolitionist one, I believe it encourages mutually beneficial relationships between humans and animals, which are seemingly denied in Regan's account.

Bernard Rollin and Teleology

Bernard Rollin (2006) is more in agreement with Regan's views than with Singer's. He rejects a utilitarian view of animal ethics for the same reasons Regan does, namely, that individuals have value in themselves and are not simply receptacles of interests. Rollin argues that animals, with interests, are ends in themselves, and that makes them objects of moral concern. To have interests as opposed to simply having needs (like plants), conscious awareness is required. He argues that for an animal to care about whether or not its needs are met, some kind of mental life, however rudimentary, is needed. Not only are pain and pleasure indicators of unmet needs, but so too are "Frustration, anxiety, malaise, listlessness, boredom, and anger" (Rollin 2006, p. 102). When these kinds of emotions are demonstrated, we can be reasonably certain that the animal has interests, not only needs, that are not being met. Rollin provides a list of the kinds of evidence we have for believing that animals are conscious, which is very similar to what I have argued for in Chap. 3. He includes neurophysiological, biochemical, and behavioural research, the presence of sense organs, and evolutionary theory, as sources of evidence for consciousness in animals (Rollin 2006).

Rollin argues that morality is fundamentally concerned with respect for an individual's interests regardless of whether it is a human or an animal. He summarizes the main claims in his argument as follows:

> It is enough that we, as moral agents, can sensibly assert that the spider has interests, which are conditions without which the creature, first of all, cannot live or, second of all, cannot live its life as a spider, cannot fulfill its *telos*. And thirdly, and most important, as we shall shortly discuss, it is necessary that we can say sensibly of the animal that it is *aware* of its struggle to live its life, that the fulfilling or thwarting of its needs *matter* to it. (Once again, we must stress that a man may not be conscious of his need for oxygen, but thwarting that need certainly *matters* to him. This sort of talk is senseless *vis-à-vis* a rock.) Further we are aware that it is in our power to nurture or impede these needs and even to destroy the entire nexus of needs and activities that constitute its life. And once this is recognized, it is difficult to see why the entire machinery of moral concern is not relevant here, for it is the

awareness of interesting living (human) beings that we have argued is constitutive of morality in the first place. (Rollin 1992, p. 75)

He later states, "Thus we have tried to argue that any living thing, insofar as it evidences interests, with or without the ability to suffer, is worthy of being an object of moral concern. Insofar as we can inform ourselves of the interests of a creature, we must at least look at that creature with moral categories." (1992, p. 79). This means that when we evaluate our actions towards animals, we must take into consideration the interests that they have and whether or not we are respecting or disrespecting them. This would be the same for both humans and animals, to the extent that they share the possession of consciousness and interests, even at the most minimal level. It does not, however, mean that all species have the same kinds of interests. Rollin admits, similarly to Singer, that the more complex the level of awareness or consciousness that an animal has, the more valuable it is in terms of moral consideration and the right to life. Although he admits it would not be clear how to deal with conflicting interests, both in situations between different animals, and between humans and other animals. He suggests that, rather than performing a utilitarian calculus, we must consider each situation individually, and resolve it dialectically.

Indeed, Rollin favours a Kantian view over that of utilitarianism, as he takes it as support for his view that all conscious animals have an intrinsic value. Rollin argues that animals are ends in themselves, and that "any living thing with interests is an end in itself, worthy of moral consideration merely in virtue of its being alive. That in turn means that even if we use another living creature as a means, it must never be merely as a means, but we should always keep in mind a respect for its end, that is, its life, and the interests and needs associated with that life that matter to it." (1992, p. 89). According to Rollin, it is not rationality that makes someone worthy of moral consideration, but conscious life that possesses interests. This is important as, for Rollin, we do not need to be abolitionists to respect the rights that animals have, as long as we do not treat animals merely as a means to our own ends. For him, this would mean that zoos are acceptable as long as animals are provided with an environment that allows for their interests to be met. For example, giraffes should have plenty of space to stand up fully and stretch their necks, and social animals should never be kept in isolation. In this way, rights are not absolute for animals, just as they are not absolute for humans, as they can be overridden in certain cases. He just wants to emphasize that when we do use animals, we use them with their intrinsic value and interests in mind.

In determining exactly what kinds of moral obligations we have towards animals, Rollin (2006) claims that the telos of an animal informs us of the specific ways that we can respect creatures belonging to different species. Telos, for living animals, is intrinsic to them as members of a particular species, or part of the genetic makeup that gives members of different species their distinctive features. This is different from the telos of a car or man-made object as in these cases it is extrinsic to the object as a result of it being conceived of and created by someone else. For example, Rollin says regarding a spider, that "it has what Aristotle called a telos, a nature, a function, a set of activities intrinsic to it, evolutionarily determined and genetically imprinted, that constitute its living spiderness" (2006, p. 100). The specific kinds of moral obligations we have towards animals are provided by the nature of the specific interests each species possesses in virtue of its own telos. He claims that:

> If the life of an animal has intrinsic value and should be weighed in our moral deliberations, so too, should its interests, which is to say its nature or telos. Indeed, it is the existence of interests that makes something a moral object in the first place. So I am now explicitly suggesting that the essence of our substantive moral obligations to animals is that any animal has a right to the kind of life that its nature dictates. In short, I am arguing that an animal has the right to have the unique interests that characterize it morally considered in our treatment of it. (Rollin 1992, p. 90)

This results in basic, common sense conclusions regarding the treatment of animals in terms of things like not keeping birds in cages too small to fly or stretch their wings in, but also in larger, more radical conclusions that challenge the uses of animals in agriculture, entertainment, and research as whole industries. To treat an animal in accordance with their telos is to respect the rights they have by virtue of their natures. For example, to keep a social animal in isolation would be wrong, as it would violate their right, as social creatures, to experience the company of other animals. To keep a bird in a cage, as a pet or in a zoo, would also violate the rights birds have by virtue of their flying nature to fulfil those interests specific to their telos.

Rollin admits that there are obvious problems with using the terms telos or nature, as it has repeatedly been abused to justify the harmful treatment of others, such as oppression of those of other races or genders. But he defends his view by pointing out that the sciences we use to learn about various species, such as ethology and biology, allow us to form accurate views on the features of various species. In this view, the increasing body of knowledge on animals and their species-specific traits creates the opportunity for greater accuracy in our moral treatment of animals.

Rollin's argument then is twofold: first, that animals are creatures that are ends in themselves by virtue of having interests that matter to them, which can be harmed or benefited by the moral actions of humans; and second, that we can identify the specific ways we ought to treat animals by understanding their telos. While I agree that animals should not be treated merely as a means to an ends for humans, using the concept of telos to determine the morality of our specific actions towards animals is problematic in ways that Rollin does not admit to. Although he admits to problems with the use of telos in the past to justify harms committed to various groups, he dismisses these objections by simply saying that we ought to be more careful when we employ the concept.

He also claims that there are concerns about how the science is actually performed that informs us of this telos. For, he argues, if science is performed dispassionately then it will ignore or deny the needs or interests of animals as such. He argues that science should be performed with an empathetic understanding of the natures of animals for it to provide us with the requisite knowledge we need to extract moral prescriptions from it. He refers to a gestalt shift that is required to see animals with the kind of moral value he ascribes to them, and that this shift is needed in science for it to be a source of knowledge concerning the telos of creatures (Rollin 1992, pp. 92–95).

This raises two problems that my view on selfhood and autonomy avoids. First, to require science itself, and its methods, to undergo a gestalt shift from dispassionate, quantitative research to empathetic understanding of the telos of animals is unreasonable given the constraints and conditions under which science is understood and performed. While I appreciate the sentiment of this kind of shift in thinking on a large scale, it is also important to keep in mind the need for knowledge and research that attempts to eliminate bias for the sake of greater truth. Too much empathy or subjective influence can also have a negative impact on science, and can lead to results that could be harmful to animals, through such things as the inaccurate or unchallenged interpretation of animal behaviours or actions. While a certain amount of anthropomorphism, for example, is inevitable in science that is focused on the study of animals, it must be carefully justified with empirical data to avoid mistaken or false conclusions regarding the natures of various creatures. If we make the mistake of being overly sentimental in our observations of animal behaviour, then we risk compromising the standards of objectivity in science, which, while they are not completely immune to personal bias or influence, still serve to ensure greater access to true knowledge.

Second, the reliance on telos as a concept that dictates moral behaviour is overly complicated and can detract from the more fundamental moral concepts, like autonomy, that are already established. Because telos can be subject to such extensive debate and criticism, it tends to lead people away from the more fundamental issues of why we owe animals moral obligations at all. In my view, minimal selfhood and autonomy provide the grounds for our moral obligations towards animals, and these concepts are what we already use to understand morality in general. Telos across species will be distinctly different for every animal we attempt to analyze, whereas minimal selfhood and autonomy are features that are universal to conscious creatures, regardless of species. Certainly selfhood and agency will manifest different behaviours and traits in different species, but they are shared features that simply exist in varying degrees across species, which provides a common ground for both science and morality. Telos is much more elusive than selfhood or agency, and more difficult to identify with any level of certainty. We assume that all birds with wings are meant to fly, but this is not necessarily the case with all birds. So, while the concept can be generally helpful, there are dangers in making unsupported assumptions about the telos of various species that could result in their mistreatment, or in actions that could harm rather than benefit that species. By focusing on the autonomy of animals, we can avoid these problems by focusing on the traits possessed by individuals that may vary from animal to animal. Telos seems more applicable to identifying traits that are characteristics of species as a whole, but it is not as applicable to unique individuals, and that might mean that we overlook an individual's specific traits, due to their own history or context, which are morally relevant to the ways we should respect their autonomy.

As a result of this problem, my view seems more plausible as there are more evidence and methods for investigating minimal selfhood than for the telos of any particular species. As we attempt to gain an understanding of "what it is like" for individuals of various species, we gain more accurate knowledge and insight into what actions will benefit or harm them. My view also provides a method for evaluating the weight of the moral obligations we owe different species, as the more minimal sense of self would require less of us, morally speaking, for a crab than for pigs, for example. This is not clearly addressed by Rollin, although I suspect it would amount to a form of interest calculus similar to Singer's view (see Tzachi Zamir 2007, for such an argument). As I argued in Chap. 4, autonomy provides us with the strongest grounds for the moral consideration of animals and, combined with the emphasis placed on the importance of selfhood, it offers a more precise guide to how we ought to treat animals than Rollin's account.

Lori Gruen and Entangled Empathy

Lori Gruen (2015) provides an alternative ethic that is based on the kinds of relationships we have with animals, rather than an ethic based on principles, such as the utilitarian and rights views examined above. Instead of looking for a specific mental capacity that animals share with humans, the approach taken by Gruen focuses on the ways in which our specific relationships with animals affect how we interact with them as individuals. She believes that in basing animal ethics on the similarities that we share with other animals, we tend to overlook the differences that make individuals valuable both to us and for themselves. It also, according to

Gruen, results in a human-oriented framework being imposed on the lives of animals, which denies or occludes the characteristics or traits that make them unique. As her view is based on a feminist ethic of care, difference is emphasized as something we ought to attend to in all of our relationships, so that we maintain a more accurate understanding of the socio-cultural inequalities in power that characterize our interactions with animals, in terms of how we use and exploit them as resources for our use. Relational and care ethics, and specifically Gruen's view of entangled ethics, try to achieve greater justice for animals, while also promoting relationships based on care and compassion. Part of Gruen's focus is to establish the problems within traditional ethical theories both in general and as they are applied to animals, to demonstrate the need for an alternative ethic for animals. As this critique is grounded in a larger feminist analysis of ethical theory in general, it is important to first attend to the reasons she provides for claiming that traditional ethical theories are inadequate as they are extended towards animals.

An important part of the feminist critique of traditional ethics is based on the idea that abstract reasoning about moral principles and ethical concepts works to detach us from the actual situations and experiences we encounter in real life. This alienation from the people and relationships we must make moral decisions about is problematic as it can erase the complexity of moral problems and moral experiences. This can result in blinding us to the many different ways moral problems can be resolved, and so limits our moral imagination. Abstraction can also be a problem as it can lead to the creation and perpetuation of conceptual binaries, where one side is valued more than the other for no good or justifiable reason. In terms of traditional ethics, one such binary exists between reason and emotion, and Gruen argues that:

> Importantly, reason and emotion cannot meaningfully be separated either, as they are mutually informing. Any compelling moral theory has to recognize that cognition/reason and affect/emotion cannot be disentangled. Rather than generating distance between us and them, justice and care, we need a theory that bridges perceived gaps between reason/emotion or self/other by recognizing the ways that each side of the bridge shapes the other without collapsing into it. (2015, pp. 34–35)

Insofar as traditional ethical theories focus on abstract, rational principles as the basis for extensionist arguments to include animals, they negate the importance of emotion and care in our relationships with other animals, by placing an emphasis on the similarities between us rather than the differences. This happens because traditional ethical theories are anthropocentric and, as such, they place a human-oriented perspective on our relationships, which means that we fail to see moral situations from an animal's own perspective. Gruen argues that having empathy for animals can help us overcome this problem, as it allows us to better grasp the peculiarities of an animal's situation and leads to a more ethically informed relationship with them (2015, p. 24).

Gruen defines entangled empathy as:

> A type of caring perception focused on attending to another's experience of wellbeing. An experiential process involving a blend of emotion and cognition in which we recognize we are in relationships with others and are called upon to be responsive and responsible in these relationships by attending to another's needs, interests, desires, vulnerabilities, hopes, and sensitivities. (2015, p. 3)

From this viewpoint, an individual is understood as part of various relationships that exist within a broader social and cultural context, and not as an autonomous and independent being. The self is seen not as an abstraction, but rather as situated within relationships that co-constitute our identities with other humans and with animals. For Gruen, the abstract self implies that we are able to extract ourselves from the contexts of our various relationships, but our experiences show us that this is an impossible task. Instead, we ought to focus on better perceiving and responding to the complex and entangled relationships we exist within (2015, pp. 63–64). To do this, she argues that we must empathize with others by trying our best to understand what it is like to experience the world from their different perspectives. She acknowledges that while there can be challenges to putting this into practice, it is possible to cognitively reflect on, and emotionally engage with, the perspectives of others. Gruen (2015) supports this, arguing:

Entangled empathy is a way for oneself to perceive and to connect with a specific other in their particular circumstance, and to recognize and assess one's place in reference to the other. This is a central skill for being in ethical relations. Entangled empathy with other animals involves reflecting on proximity and distance. To do it well we have to try to understand the individual's species-typical behaviors and her individual personality over a period of time. Very often this is not easy to do without expertise and observation. Many, perhaps most, current discussions of what we owe animals fail to attend to the particularity of individual animal lives and the very different sorts of relationships we are in with them. The category "animal" itself obscures important differences and relationships. Chickens, chipmunks, and chimpanzees are animals, but we are in different types of relationships with each. Particular relationships with chimpanzees give us virtually no context for understanding and empathizing with chickens and the same holds true for chipmunks. Theories that generalize over differences will obscure the distinct experiences of others. (67)

So, to practice entangled empathy requires not only knowledge about species and the general sorts of traits they possess, but it also requires a recognition of how humans interact with individuals of those species. Depending on the specific nature of those relationships, how we ought to treat them needs to be informed by an awareness of how those types of relationship affect both our understanding of those animals, and our ability to empathize with them. For example, we are most likely to empathize fairly easily with companion animals like dogs and cats, whereas it will be more difficult to empathize with pigs, who are considered generally to be agricultural or farm animals used for food. By reflecting on the differences between the very nature of these types of relationships, we can ask ourselves why we might value the relationships we have with companion animals more than those we have, or do not have, with agricultural animals. When some people become educated about the cognitive capacities and species-related traits of pigs in comparison to those of dogs, for example, they may re-evaluate their views on how pigs ought to be treated, and view them with more empathy than they had previously considered. For Gruen, theories that fail to identify and emphasize the differences between various individual animals and species reduce and obscure the value of the experiences that animals actually have.

Gruen's view presents a few important challenges to my own, as I have focused on the importance of cognitive capacities for determining moral consideration, and I have posited the moral concept of autonomy as a basis for animal ethics, which is used in traditional ethical theories like Kantianism, which she rejects. I want to address these challenges, and also consider the possibility that my own view can be applied in conjunction with a relational ethic like entangled empathy. The first challenge raised by Gruen's view is that by basing animal ethics on capacities that are similar to our own, we run the risk of obscuring important differences between species and individual animals. This can result in neglecting the nature of our distinct relationships with different kinds of animals, and denying the importance of the experiences that other animals have. The focus of traditional ethical theories is to apply abstract, rational principles to our actions and moral decisions. This often comes with the cost of ignoring our emotional responses to specific situations and individuals we are trying to make moral decisions about. I agree that this is a problem, and that it is based on a broader social and cultural context which tends to value reason over emotion. Ethical decisions are, and should be, informed by both reason and emotion. However, when faced with providing a justification for why we ought to radically alter our current treatment of animals to the broader population, including individual citizens, consumers, and industries that exploit animals on a vast scale for food and research purposes, it seems riskier to me to rely on an empathetic response to the experiences of animals than it does to provide a cumulative body of evidence in the form of scientific research and arguments which show that animals experience the world in ways similar to humans. People may be more likely to enter into individual relationships with animals they have not previously encountered based on an increased understanding and curiosity about the minds of animals and the mental capacities they possess. Providing them with further arguments that link those capacities with reasons why animals are morally relevant to evaluating our interactions with them allows them to make the logical connection between what we know about animals and, as a result, how we ought to treat them.

Singer, for example, provides arguments to support the idea that animals suffer, and that suffering matters morally. He does this by showing that suffering is a capacity shared by animals and humans, and that to ignore this based on the idea of human superiority is akin to unjust discrimination like racism and sexism. While Gruen by no means denies the value of Singer's arguments and the importance of suffering, she seems to want to reject the whole view for failing to recognize the importance of individual relationships we have with animals and the role empathy and emotions play in determining the right way to treat them. However, I believe that the failings of Singer's and utilitarian views of ethics generally is that they deny the importance of autonomy by neglecting to account for some animals being intentional, self-aware agents. These capacities not only provide the grounds for claiming that animals can be more or less autonomous, but also that they are the kinds of beings we can empathize with. And so, although Gruen claims that the abstract self posited by traditional ethical theories can lead to a denial of the importance of the relationships we are embedded in, I believe that our views are compatible in the sense that my view does not preclude the notion that autonomous agents do not exist outside of these relationships. Gruen argues that her view is limited to sentient beings who have experiences (2015, p. 67), and I would agree with her and further claim that this admits to the importance of understanding and acknowledging the similarities that exist between humans and animals in terms of agency and self-awareness. The existence of an animal self is assumed by Gruen for it to be the kind of creature we can empathize with in the first place, but the problem is that not all people share in this assumption. The idea that most animals are self-aware needs to be supported and justified, and research into animal minds and the concept of self-awareness provides the basis for the caring relationships Gruen calls for. Using these mental capacities as the basis of an animal ethic grounded in autonomy does not deny the importance of individual relationships, but rather it calls for greater and more careful consideration as to how our relationships affect or reduce the autonomy of other individual animals. The first step towards this is made by establishing the reasons why animals are selves that have value, both for them and for us.

Conclusion

Singer, Regan, Rollin, and Gruen provide detailed and complex arguments in favour of the moral consideration of animals from different moral perspectives. In this chapter I have provided an overview of their arguments along with some of the main challenges these theories face when they are applied to animals. Utilitarianism and rights views do not tend to value the autonomy or selfhood of individual animals to the extent needed to overcome moral problems that arise when the interests of humans and other animals conflict. The value and autonomy of individual animals can also be too easily overridden by a focus on the interests or telos of larger groups of animal or species. I believe Gruen's view of entangled empathy can work in conjunction with my own view of autonomy, despite her rejection of traditional ethical theories and concepts, especially in our relationships with animals. In the next chapter I consider Kantian views on animals, and their modern reinterpretations, as further sources of support for the claim that animals are acting, self-aware, and autonomous agents.

References

Cavalieri, P. (2001). *The animal question: Why nonhuman animals deserve human rights*. New York: Oxford University Press.

Francione, G. L. (2008). *Animals as persons: Essays on the abolition of animal exploitation*. New York: Columbia University Press.

Franklin, J. H. (2005). *Animal rights and moral philosophy*. New York: Columbia University Press.

Frey, R. G. (1980). *Interests and rights: The case against animals*. Oxford: Clarendon Press.

Garner, R. (2005a). *Animal ethics*. Malden: Polity Press.

Garner, R. (2005b). *The political theory of animal rights*. New York: Manchester University Press.

Gruen, L. (2015). *Entangled empathy: An alternative ethic for our relationship with animals*. New York: Lantern Books.

Pluhar, E. B. (1995). *Beyond prejudice: The moral significance of human and non-human animals.* Durham: Duke University Press.

Regan, T. (1983). *The case for animal rights.* Berkeley: University of California Press.

Regan, T. (2001). *Defending animal rights.* Chicago: University of Illinois Press.

Regan, T. (2004). *Empty cages: Facing the challenge of animal rights.* Toronto: Rowman & Littlefield.

Rollin, B. E. (1992). *Animal rights and human morality.* New York: Prometheus Books.

Rollin, B. E. (2006). *Animal rights and human morality* (3rd ed.). Amherst: Prometheus Books.

Rowlands, M. (2009). *Animal rights: Moral theory and practice* (2nd ed.). New York: Palgrave MacMillan.

Singer, P. (1993). *Practical ethics* (2nd ed.). New York: Cambridge University Press.

Zamir, T. (2007). *Ethics and the beast: A speciesist argument for animal liberation.* Princeton: Princeton University Press.

6

Kantian Ethics and Animals

Introduction

In Chap. 5, I presented four of the main positions in animal ethics, represented by Singer, Regan, Rollin, and Gruen. These positions all provide arguments and specific criteria with which to grant moral consideration to animals. However, I argue that agency, selfhood, and autonomy provide stronger foundations for a theory of animal ethics than these four views, as they stand. As Kantian moral theory places such importance on freedom and respect for autonomy, a more thorough investigation of how this theory could provide support for my own view is warranted. At first glance this could be seen as problematic since Kant himself believed that animals are only owed indirect moral duties, as they do not qualify as autonomous persons by his account. Recent reinterpretations of Kant present alternative readings of his arguments in the attempt to support direct moral duties towards animals, and I argue that these create the best moral foundation for my own view.

In this chapter I present a brief summary of Kant's view regarding animals, and a more in-depth examination of three particular attempts, by Wright, Wood, and Korsgaard, to reinterpret his views to support direct moral duties towards animals. Although not without problems, these three views provide good reasons for why we ought to value animals as ends in themselves. I argue that the inclusion of agency and selfhood can further strengthen these three positions while attempting to preserve the integrity and consistency of the main claims in Kant's own arguments.

Kant on Animals

Kantian moral theory has generally been interpreted to provide an account of indirect moral obligations towards animals. This means that animals are only morally considerable insofar as our treatment of them reflects on our own moral character, either cultivating cruel and mean behaviours or kind and compassionate ones. We do not, according to Immanuel Kant (1964), owe animals direct moral obligations as they do not share our rational nature, which is the requirement for status as an autonomous, moral person. Having a rational nature gives someone the status of an end in themselves, to be treated accordingly as an end and never purely as a means to an end. Kant is clear that "Beings whose existence depends, not on our will, but on nature, have none the less, if they are non-rational beings, only a relative value as means and are consequently called things. Rational beings, on the other hand, are called persons because their nature already marks them out as ends in themselves." (Kant 1964, p. 96) Indeed, his views on animals and their proper treatment are quite clearly indicated in this passage. Animals are not, according to Kant, ends in themselves, and have value only as things that can contribute to our own moral growth as humans. This view is further explained when Kant says:

> But so far as animals are concerned, we have no direct duties. Animals are not self-conscious and are there merely as a means to an end. That end is man…Our duties towards animals are merely indirect duties towards humanity. Animal nature has analogies to human nature, and by doing our

duties to animals in respect of manifestations which correspond to manifestations of human nature, we indirectly do our duty towards humanity. Thus, if a dog has served his master long and faithfully, his service, on the analogy of human service, deserves reward, and when the dog has grown too old to serve, his master ought to keep him until he dies. (1963, pp. 239–240)

From this passage, it seems safe to say that Kant has a clear position on the moral status of animals as a means only to our own ends and that they are only indirectly valuable to us through our duty to humanity. In other words, we should treat animals well in order to learn how to treat other humans well, as it encourages us to develop respect more generally, and as we have a direct duty to treat other humans with respect, this is beneficial to our moral development.

J. Skidmore (2001) provides a useful summary of Kant's first and second formulations of the categorical imperative, which clearly indicate that animals are not to be considered as rational ends, towards whom we have direct moral duties. The first formulation of the categorical imperative tells us to act in such a way as to treat humanity, in ourselves and in others, as an end and never simply as a means. The second formulation of the categorical imperative follows from the first, and it commands us to treat the rational agency in a person as an end in itself. All other beings, as they are non-rational, are things or objects that can be treated as means to our own ends. In explaining how these two formulations of the categorical imperative relate to animals, Skidmore (2001) writes:

> First, there are rational beings, or persons, who have an unconditional worth which he calls dignity, and as such they must be treated as ends in themselves. Second, there are all other beings, non-rational beings who have only conditional worth and thus take on the moral status of things that may be treated merely as means. This suggests that Kant's later conclusion that there are no direct duties to animals can be seen as a simple and direct application of the formula of humanity and the reasoning that leads up to it. (543)

As such, if the source of all value in Kant's theory is rational agency, and animals are not rational agents, then there is no way to argue that animals are owed direct moral consideration in this view. Only rational agents are autonomous, as they can legislate universal moral laws while also being subject to those laws. Animals clearly do not possess the mental capacities to consider, create, or endorse such universal moral laws, and so they do not belong in the kingdom of ends that Kant describes in the third formulation of the categorical imperative (Skidmore 2001, p. 543).

However, Kant does not endorse the cruel or abusive treatment of animals, and makes various claims about how we ought to treat them kindly and with consideration. He argues that we can judge humans by how they treat animals, and he prohibits the use of animals in experiments without purpose or killing for sport. Indeed, he admits that animals can feel pain, and that animals can act in ways analogous to human ways and that some of their acts "spring from the same principles" (1963, p. 240). As such, we should not overwork them, and should show them gratitude for their service to us by treating them as members of our own family. If we must kill them, it should be quickly and without suffering. After discussing why we should not wantonly destroy nature or plants for fear of destroying the propensity in man towards appreciating beauty, he says, "With regard to the animate but nonrational part of creation, violent and cruel treatment of animals is far more intimately opposed to man's duty to himself, and he has a duty to refrain from this; for it dulls his shared feeling of their pain and so weakens and gradually uproots a natural predisposition that is very serviceable to morality in one's relations with other men." (1991, p. 238) This acknowledgement by Kant of the capacities of animals for performing acts of duty, experiencing pain, and possessing feeling and choice is surprising given the time when he was writing.

As Kant did not believe that animals are rational, and thereby are not persons or moral agents, he advocated for indirect duties towards animals instead of direct ones. Some would argue that this is enough to get the kind of moral consideration towards animals that most would want, as it does require us to treat animals humanely and with compassion. Indeed, one such view is supported by Lara Denis (2000), who argues that Kantian duties regarding animals would have a large impact on our current practices involving eating and using animals for research and entertainment. These duties amount to duties towards ourselves and humanity, as she takes Kant's position, as outlined above, at face value. However, Kant's view maintains the idea that there is a distinct and categorical difference between animals and humans that is no longer supported by current evidence, as I have explained in Chaps. 2 and 3. I believe that direct moral obligations are owed to animals in virtue of their agency and selfhood, and not indirectly through the obligations we owe to other humans. Is it possible to find reasons, based on Kant's own arguments, for having direct moral obligations towards animals? Kantian ethical theory is more appealing than utilitarian views as it implies that certain actions are immoral, regardless of the possible benefits or consequences they might bring to us. And so, in what follows, I focus on three attempts to reinterpret Kant's arguments as supporting the direct moral consideration of animals.

Wright on Kant and Animal Autonomy

William Wright (1993) argues that Kant's Formula of the End-in-itself is commonly interpreted to mean that "every rational agent is committed to taking rational nature as an end, and this commitment stems from the fact that we each necessarily view our own rational nature as an end" (1993, p. 356). When we find this rational nature in others, we must also take it as an end, and this exists only in other human beings. Wright contends that what is meant by rational nature is up for debate by post-Kantians, and that there are three ways to interpret it. First, there is the *strict autonomy view*, which says if someone has a rational nature they must always act in accordance with the moral law. Wright rejects this option as a satisfactory definition of rational nature as we all know that people do not have fully rational natures, and that we often act based on other desires or impulses. And so, second, there is the *positive freedom view*, which suggests rational nature simply means that we have the ability to act for reasons that we can evaluate, according to the categorical imperative. This implies that we do not always act morally, but that we strive to live according to certain moral standards. The third and final view of rational nature is the one Wright endorses, which he calls the *negative freedom view*. This view requires only that someone possess the ability to make choices, voluntarily and with intentions. As he describes it, "The point is only that a being with a rational nature is one who acts voluntarily, with intentions that can be captured in maxims, and whose maxims need not refer to his or her desires or inclinations. This position is weaker than the positive freedom view in that it requires only the ability to make choices; it does not require any evaluation of those choices." (Wright 1993, p. 357). Wright believes that in the negative freedom view, and according to Kant's own arguments, only choice is properly understood as free, whereas the will is not. The will is concerned with evaluating reasons for or against an action, but choice implies the ability to act freely. So, for Wright, having freedom of choice is sufficient for possessing a rational nature. Also, in the positive freedom view, we are only obligated to treat others as ends if they are capable of appraising the morality of their own actions. However, small children and the intellectually disabled are incapable of doing this, and so in the positive freedom view, they do not count as members in the kingdom of ends (Wright 1993, p. 358). This is a common problem for Kantian moral theory, and by endorsing the negative freedom view Wright provides grounds for direct moral obligations towards marginal humans and animals. For, as he suggests, if the idea that animals can make choices can be supported with evidence, then they too possess rational nature, according to the negative freedom view, and are ends in themselves deserving of moral consideration. This is because, according to Wright:

> In the course of deliberating about what to do, everyone necessarily views herself or himself as able to make choices independently of desires or coercion. This ability is the end of their actions in the sense of being a ground of action, not in the sense of being something produced or following from the action. The same ability is manifested in others as they deliberate, and consistency requires that what grounds our actions must be treated with equal respect wherever it appears. Consequently, we must never treat rational nature wherever it appears merely as a means but always as an end. (1993, pp. 358–359)

This is very similar to part of Christine Korsgaard's (2012) argument (which is examined later in this chapter), where she claims that it is the choice for a desired end that is more important than the consequent rational reflection on it, in terms of what obligates us towards others. That is, to universalize a maxim into moral law, we must first make a choice about which end to pursue, and then rationalize it into a moral law. But this does not mean the rational reflection about that choice obligates us more than the initial choice itself, as the initial choice indicates that the creature to which it belongs must be a creature with interests, and to whom things matter (good or bad). It is to creatures that can make choices about what is good or bad for them that we owe direct moral obligations, and that includes animals and marginal humans, for both Wright and Korsgaard.

For Wright to support his claim that animals can make choices, he refers to a couple of animal behavioural scientists who discuss animal play, the use of tools, and deception. His argument is that there is enough scientific evidence to support the claim that animals have the mental representations necessary to make decisions about goals and activities. He argues that "Without mental representations of possible goals, and of actions or objects required to reach the goals, no being could make choices in the same sense that humans do" (Wright 1993, p. 360). He also supports the view that animals are conscious using arguments from evolutionary continuity and the principle of parsimony in interpreting animal behaviour. He does not believe, however, that it is necessary to show that animals are self-conscious, as he believes that making choices does not require it. He argues that only at the level of evaluating choices is self-consciousness needed, and that if animals are conscious, then they are able to make choices and thus meet the criteria for being morally considerable (Wright 1993, pp. 359–361).

He further specifies that animals are to be considered as conscious and capable of making choices including higher primates, and domesticated animals that are kept as pets and companions. He suggests that the ability of animals we raise for food falls into a grey area in terms of their capacity to make choices, and says that, "Chickens seem to pursue only food and survival, and we seldom speak as if they choose to act as they do. We should not put too much emphasis on how we happen to interpret animals' behavior, but the clear cases of animals to be respected in all our actions are those who meet both conditions: (1) their actions are easily interpreted as resulting from choices, and (2) they are conscious (according to our best arguments)." (Wright 1993, p. 362). He concludes his argument with examples of how we ought to treat animals according to his view, which basically amounts to treating animals as ends, and not merely as means to our own ends. And so, we not only have an obligation to protect the negative freedoms that animals might have to not be hurt, but we are also obligated to try to increase their happiness and preserve their natural habitats.

Wright's account of rational nature as the ability to make choices preserves the strength of Kant's categorical imperative and provides a strong foundation for valuing the autonomy of others wherever we find it. In my view, minimal autonomy is similar to Wright's negative freedom view in the sense that what is morally important is an individual's ability to control their own actions and pursue their own ends. Although Wright does not discuss in much detail the relation between his conception of rational nature and autonomy, I believe that it is important to emphasize that autonomy should not be considered as only possible through the use of rational reflection. Rationality is simply to act on the basis of reasons, even if those reasons are minimally complex. Choices themselves will be increasingly complex, to the extent that an animal is capable of higher reasoning capacities. To acknowledge that choice requires freedom means that in order to respect someone's autonomy one is obligated to allow individuals to make their own choices, to the greatest extent possible. This applies to both moral agents and moral patients (as Wright and Korsgaard would agree), which is where my own view would differ from Kant's. As most animals can be considered to be at least minimally rational, then they are also minimally autonomous.

Wright's dismissal of the importance of self-consciousness does not affect the strength of his argument as a whole, but it does conflict with my own view that to be conscious is to be aware of one's own experiences, and this means that the creature in question is self-aware, even if only minimally so. My own view of agency and self-consciousness allows for a more complex account of the degree to which we owe various species moral obligations, as minimal self-consciousness and minimal agency imply minimal autonomy. It also strengthens the underlying reasons why someone ought to be considered morally valuable, as it is only by being self-aware that someone can care about what happens to them. That is, only self-aware creatures who are agents, even minimally, experience what happens to them, which gives rise to preferences and desires, for example, and so it is by virtue of this self-awareness that they can be ends in themselves. Respecting the autonomy of an individual follows from the value of selfhood, even if only minimally, and Wright's view omits this connection.

Also, Wright seems to be suggesting that very few species would qualify for inclusion in the moral community, and he favours species the average person would perceive as being able to make rational choices. This does not reflect an awareness of the scientific sources that include birds and fish, for example, along with many other species, as creatures that possess beliefs, desires, preferences, and self-awareness. For example, just by focusing on one area of research, animal welfare science, we can see that chickens, pigs, and cows (what Wright terms food animals) have clear preferences that go beyond food and survival. To improve the welfare of farm animals, many studies have shown that allowing animals to build nests, socialize with other animals, and providing them with choices for living conditions demonstrates that these animals too possess rational natures by Wright's own account (see Druce and Lymbery 2006, for examples of improving the welfare of farm animals). If they did not, the entire field of animal welfare science would be redundant. As such, it seems conspicuous that Wright places an emphasis on higher primates, to whom humans are perceived to be "closest" in terms of their traits, and companion animals, with whom we generally have the closest emotional bonds. As there is so much at stake for the animals themselves, it seems odd that Wright would state that we should not place too much emphasis on interpreting animal behaviours as conscious or as making choices. If they are ends in themselves, or potentially so, then morally it would make more sense to err on the side of caution and interpret animal behaviours generously in favour of consciousness and self-awareness, rather than too stringently. The body of research on animal minds shows us that, broadly speaking, many, if not most, animals possess the mental capacities required for self-awareness and the ability to make their own choices. And so, decisions about which species count as rational and deserving of treatment as ends in themselves should be based on their mental capacities for rationality and self-awareness, rather than on the benefits they might provide us with through their use.

Wood on Kant and Rational Nature

Allen W. Wood (1998) provides another reinterpretation of Kant's arguments regarding who is owed direct moral consideration as ends, by claiming that we should understand Kant's command to respect rational nature in individual persons as a command to respect rational nature in the abstract, which includes anyone who possesses fragments or parts of it, the necessary conditions for it, who has had it in the past, or the potential for it (197). Wood supports this view by saying that, for Kant, our obligations towards other rational agents are grounded in what he calls the personification principle. This means that we owe respect to the rational nature in other particular persons as instances of it. As animals are not persons, as they lack rational nature, we do not, in Kant's view, owe them direct moral duties. He explains this point by saying:

> As we have seen, Kant regards only rational beings as *persons*, which are to be treated as ends, regarding all other beings as *things*. Even his statement of the Formula of Humanity as End in Itself—"*So act that you use humanity, whether in your own person or in the person of any other, always at the same time as an end, never merely as a means*" (G 4:429)—involves the idea that humanity or rational nature has a claim on us only in the person of a being who actually possesses it. This idea is what I will call the *personification principle*. (1998, p. 193)

This, for Wood, is not satisfactory as it does not reflect the fact that most of us do value the welfare of other living beings for their own sake, and not just for the betterment of our own moral development. He argues that to respect rational nature as an end in itself sometimes requires us to, "behave with respect toward nonrational beings if they bear the right relations to rational nature." (Wood 1998, p. 197). And so, this is why he believes that we ought to respect rational nature in the abstract, in terms of those beings who possess fragments of it, even if they are not fully rational themselves. As children and humans whose mental abilities have been compromised in various ways are not fully rational, in Kantian terms, it does not follow that we ought to treat them merely as means or as things. Indeed, he believes that to treat these sorts of humans in this way is showing contempt for rational nature, as it can result in neglecting them or caring about those parts of rational nature they do possess (Wood 1998, p. 198). This also applies to animals, as Wood argues that they possess recognizable fragments of rational nature, in terms of the capacities they have for desires and the ability to experience pleasure or pain. He also refers to Regan's notion of preference autonomy, as the ability to initiate actions and to have preferences, as a necessary condition for rational autonomy that animals possess. And so, the capacities that animals have provide the "infrastructure" of our own rational nature, and this means that we owe them respect and direct moral consideration.

Whereas Wright's reinterpretation of Kant's arguments focuses on the concept of autonomy, Wood's view focuses on Kant's view of rational nature. It seems that their views do not conflict, as they both acknowledge that many animals possess certain mental capacities that constitute rationality, at least minimally. Wood, however, argues that preference autonomy, as the ability to initiate actions and have preferences, is a necessary condition for the rational autonomy on which Kantian ethics is grounded. He does not seem to believe that autonomy exists in degrees, or that minimal autonomy is itself valuable and the source of direct moral obligations. Some (Skidmore 2001; Korsgaard 2006) would argue that autonomy in Kant's theory is only possessed by fully rational humans, and that you either possess the ability to evaluate your moral reasons for acting and to legislate moral laws, or you do not. Autonomy does not admit to degrees, and fragments of it or alternate versions of it, like the negative freedom view that Wright endorses, are not reflective of the dignity it provides humanity with. Skidmore, for example, claims, "For it is autonomy, the capacity to set ends and pursue them independently of desire, the capacity to obey categorical imperatives, that makes moral agency possible" (2001, p. 545). He believes that animals do not possess the mental capacities to perform such actions at all, and as such, they cannot be understood as ends in themselves, despite the argument Wood provides in favour of respecting aspects of rational nature. It is possible that if Wood provides a stronger and more thorough account of the rational capacities that animals possess, his own argument would be more convincing to critics like Skidmore. In my own view, providing a more detailed account of the mental capacities of animals which allows them to be considered as intentional agents and as self-aware provides the grounds for arguing that autonomy is best understood as existing in both minimal and rich forms. Using this line of reasoning, it would be possible to argue that rational nature itself admits to degrees, with animals being more or less able to evaluate their reasons for acting. This is supported by the views presented in Chap. 2, which claim that animals can be considered moral subjects whose emotions count as reasons for acting, and as minimal moral agents. Because Wood is not arguing that animals possess rational nature itself, it is possible to object to his view by asking why the infrastructure for rational nature is to be taken as valuable. This is because there are other possible capacities that could be part of the infrastructure of rational nature, other than desire and the ability to experience pleasure or pain, which we do not view as necessarily valuable. So if we can argue instead that there is such a thing as a minimally rational nature which is possessed by animals, small children, and so on, then we can base our respect for animals on that as it grants animals the status of being minimally autonomous.

Korsgaard on Kant and Animal Nature

Christine Korsgaard (2005) challenges the standard interpretation of Kant's position on animals, saying that not only does she think it is possible to provide an account of direct moral duties to animals using Kant's theories, but that he himself did not see the implications of his own argument and how it could be used to support such a position. Korsgaard posits that animals are also ends in themselves by virtue of what she calls their animal nature, which is also shared by humans. Korsgaard begins her argument by stating that her overall goal is to find within Kant's own arguments the "ground of our obligations to the other animals" (2005, p. 82). She is intent on showing that although Kant argues that direct moral duties are only properly bestowed on rational human agents as a result of their ability "to regulate their conduct in accordance with an assessment of their principles", it does not follow that we have no moral obligations to animals (2005, p. 87). In fact, she argues that animals are ends in themselves, and thus deserving of direct moral obligations based on an account of animal nature that, while reflecting Kant's original definition of animal nature, reinterprets it in a novel way.

Korsgaard gives an account of Kant's argument regarding the status of ends in themselves as rational, human beings. She says that the key characteristic of a rational end in itself is the legislative will. It is only humans as "rational animals, by contrast, that think about and therefore assess the principles that govern our beliefs and actions" (2005, p. 86). She argues that for Kant, rationality means "the capacity for normative self-government" (87). Korsgaard also states, "Because we regulate our conduct in this way—in accordance with our own conception of laws—Kant describes us as having 'legislative wills,'... and of regulating our beliefs and actions in accordance with those judgments" (2005, p. 87). For this reason, only humans are ends in themselves, as they are the only creatures that can morally assess and regulate their conduct through their awareness and reflection on the reasons they have for acting. As animals are not conscious of the principles and reasons for the ways they act, they cannot assess them rationally, and thus do not have legislative wills, which would allow them to belong to Kant's kingdom of ends. If animals have no moral obligations to each other or to us, then Kant argues we have no obligations to them, as we cannot hold them accountable for their actions as we do with other humans. As animals cannot enter into moral contracts with us, in the form of legislating moral laws, they are not moral agents. Only moral agents, through their ability to reason and have legislative wills are worthy of direct moral consideration for Kant. Korsgaard questions this reasoning, arguing that although animals do not themselves have moral obligations towards others, it does not follow that we do not have any moral obligations to them.

Although Korsgaard agrees with Kant that animals do not have legislative wills, and thus this cannot be "the source of obligation", in the same way humans are, she does say that it does not follow that animals cannot be ends in themselves in a different sense. She argues that animals can be the source of legitimate normative claims, as they *can* obligate us (2005, pp. 95–96). In the same way that Kant's passive citizens, such as children and women, can obligate us "in the sense having a claim on him in the name of a law whose authority he acknowledges", we can choose to will into existence laws to protect non-human animals through rational reflection (2005, p. 96). Korsgaard argues that, for example, we would choose to legislate against being tortured, hunted, or eaten, not just because these things would assault our autonomous, rational nature, but rather because these things would assault our animal nature. Our animal nature, which of course is shared with other, non-rational animals, is derived from the notion that all animals have a good for themselves. This good is something that the animal is aware of and strives towards, through pursuing those things that benefit it and avoiding those that harm it. She believes that an animal has the ability to pursue what is naturally good or bad for it based on their experiences. Although animals cannot reflect on their ends as good, Korsgaard argues that:

> an animal experiences the satisfaction of its needs and the things that will satisfy them as desirable for pleasant, and assaults on its being as undesirable or unpleasant. These experiences are the basis of its incentives, making its own good the end of its actions. In that sense, an animal is an organic system to whom its own good matters...We could even say that an animal is an organic system that matters to itself, for it pursues its own good for its own sake. (2005, p. 103)

In this way Korsgaard provides an account of animal nature shared by humans and non-humans. This means that we can value our animal nature as an end in itself, which gives us a reason to extend moral obligations to animals through our legislative wills. She says that to the extent that we value things like eating, drinking, playing, and curiosity, and disvalue things like pain, loss of control, and physical mutilation, we are valuing our animal nature. When we legislate for or against these things, we are legislating on behalf of our animal nature. She argues that what Kant *really* meant was:

> Human beings...are not distinguished from the other animals by being in connection with some sort of transcendental, rational order beyond nature with which the other animals have nothing to do. Instead we are distinguished by our ability to *construct* a transcendental, rational order out of the essential love of life and the goods of life that we share with other animals. (2005, p. 105)

So, our moral obligations to other animals come from a shared state of being an end in itself, based on an animal nature which indicates that all animals pursue their own good, for their own sake. Humans are distinct from animals only in the sense that we can create value and place it on ourselves and others through our rational, legislative wills. We would not have a rational nature or legislative will, were it not for our animal nature, and thus we should take our animal nature to be an end in itself, and as a reason to extend direct moral obligations to animals.

The claim that animal nature is an end in itself and Korsgaard's explanation of what this means leads to a concern with her argument. The idea that both plants and animals have a good for themselves, along with the lack of justification for the idea that animals experience their goods in ways plants do not, raises questions as to how, exactly, humans ought to be morally obligated to animals and yet not plants. In her explanation of what animal nature is, she focuses on the idea that animals have their own goods that matter to them. Indeed, she describes the kind of good that an animal has as something that it can experience and pursue for its own sake. Plants too, have their own goods, but not in the same sense that animals do. Both plants and animals have natural goods, and they can both be said to matter to themselves. While plants have goods in the sense of having needs that can be affected by things that interfere with their functioning, animals have goods in what she says is "a deeper sense still" (Korsgaard 2005, p. 102). An animal can *experience and pursue* what is good or bad for it, in a directed, intentional sort of way that plants cannot. She also explains that the only distinction between humans and animals is the capacity for humans to reflect on those goods and ends, which is associated with rational nature rather than simply animal nature. An animal has, as its incentives, the pursuit of things that will satisfy its desires, and the avoidance of things that are undesirable. It is through the *experience* of these incentives that an animal makes its own good the end of its actions, and it pursues its own good for its own sake.

In another work, Korsgaard (2011) presents this argument in a slightly modified way, as part of a discussion about the way we legislate moral laws, and how they pertain to animals. She writes:

The stronger way to make the argument is just to say that because the original act of self-respect involves a decision to treat what is naturally good or bad for you as something good or bad objectively and normatively, the self on whom value is conferred is the self for whom things can be naturally good or bad. And the self for whom things can be naturally good or bad is your animal self: that is the morally significant thing we have in common with other animals. It is on ourselves as possessors of a natural good, that is, on our animal selves, that we confer value. Since our legislation is universal, and confers value on animal nature, it follows that we will that all animals are to be treated as ends in themselves. (Korsgaard 2011, p. 98)

The idea of natural good is what what we share with animals through our animal nature, and it is the source of our moral obligations towards them. In her discussion of natural goods she relies on the Aristotelian concept of telos to explain what she means by this. Korsgaard believes that animal nature possesses such goods as interests in the avoidance of pain, the pursuit of pleasure, and so on. But these are only valuable insomuch as they give rise to our rational natures, which allow us to be autonomous, moral agents that can legislate moral laws. So although she is arguing that animal nature is valuable in itself, it is difficult to see how she makes this connection. For if animal nature is valuable as a means to rational nature, how can it also be valuable in itself?

This problem is why she includes the argument of natural goods and telos in support of her claims. I argued in Chap. 5 that the concept of telos is ambiguous, as we are unable to provide good reasons for claiming that animals or plants have some kind of purpose or innate value specific to species. To rely on such a concept to explain why animals are owed moral consideration but plants are not does not explain why animal nature is valuable in itself. It would be better for her to omit this from her argument and focus on the idea that as conscious beings, animals experience things as good or bad for them. This is the basis of interests that matter morally, as it means that human actions can affect the fulfilment or thwarting of these interests in ways that can harm or benefit animals. Certainly, we can harm the interests of a plant to flourish, but as plants do not experience and value what happens to them, they cannot be said to be self-aware or autonomous, and thereby cannot be owed direct moral obligations.

Korsgaard considers the possible objection to her argument that only animals with a self-concept can properly be said to be the kinds of things that can matter to themselves. It is this point that raises the biggest challenge to her argument, an important part of which states there is a clear distinction between rational and animal nature, such that animals are only morally considerable as a result of the legislation of their value by rational agents themselves. The way in which Korsgaard has set up the value of animal nature indicates that we must also accept a notion of animal nature that is itself rational, which means that the kind of self animals have is differentiated from rational, human nature only by a matter of degree, not by kind. For, if the key distinction between animals and plants is that animals can experience their goods as goods, then animals must have a conscious self-awareness, even if only minimally, that allows them to identify with those goods. They must also be able to direct their actions towards ends that matter to themselves, as agents. As such, the distinction between rational human nature and non-human animal nature is not one that Korsgaard can maintain as a result of the argument she has made. This is because animals must be able to make choices about what ends they wish to pursue (as Wright describes in his negative freedom view). To be capable of this, animals must be self-aware, at least minimally, to be considered conscious at all. Clearly Korsgaard would not endorse the view of minimal selfhood that I have argued for in Chap. 3, where conscious experience requires self-awareness, even if in the most minimal sense. However, my view makes more sense of the claim that conscious and self-aware animals have interests that vary according to the complexity of the self they possess.

Returning to the claim Korsgaard considers above, that "some people will be tempted to say that only an animal with a self-conception can be said to 'matter to itself'", Korsgaard says that one problem here is finding a univocal definition of a self-concept (2005, p. 103). Granted, this is not an easy question to answer, but I think the importance of pursuing this question is underestimated by Korsgaard, both with regard to the distinction she is trying to maintain between rational and non-rational beings, and to her goal of basing direct duties to animals on the shared animal nature of humans and non-humans. And just because it might be difficult to find or develop a univocal definition of self-awareness, does not preclude it from being something we talk about, or something we can investigate. As we saw in Chap. 3, scientists already use the concept in their own research, despite the fact that there is no one, absolute definition. She also says that the self-consciousness of human beings is constructed from a conception of their inner states and activities as being their own inner states and activities, and that this comes from an ability to "situate oneself within one's inner world, identify oneself as the subject of one's own representations" (2005, p. 103). By defining selfhood only at this complex level, where someone can take their inner state as an object of reflection, she denies that there is any other way to define self-awareness at less complex levels.

As I have argued previously, animals do have minimal selfhood and the ability to identify with their own experiences. There is no good reason to posit fully reflective self-awareness as the only form of selfhood. Selfhood can include both rich and reflective self-awareness and a minimal sense of mine-ness. It would strengthen the argument for Korsgaard to accept that animal and rational nature exist on a continuum, rather than in separate categories, especially as she describes rational nature as emerging from animal nature. Korsgaard wants to maintain a clear distinction between the two, but this is not possible given that she describes rational nature as emerging from animal nature. Having a self-concept, if it means being self-aware, is a feature of animal nature that allows that animal to value (what matters to itself) and act as an agent based on its own beliefs, desires, preferences, and so on.

Although Korsgaard briefly entertains the possible analogues of self-awareness found in various studies performed on animals, including mirror self-recognition tests, the ability to respond to names when called, and the ability of social animals to locate themselves within a social hierarchy, she dismisses them as unimportant to her argument. Her response to these claims is that, according to the view she has already laid out, all animals can be said to pursue what is naturally good for them, and that this is the *only* requirement needed to make her argument work. She dismisses the need for a self-concept in animals as being what makes them directly morally considerable, on the grounds that the value animals have is conferred on them by us, rational human agents, and as such, we do not need to look for rational, autonomous behaviour in animals themselves to grant them direct moral duties. But this seems to maintain a distinction between humans and animals that is arbitrary, and not based on the evidence of minimal selfhood in animals. Also, it does not explain why we should value the ability of animals to pursue what is good for them and to act as agents. Instead, she says that it is by virtue of our shared animal nature that we can confer value on animals, and that is sufficient to achieve her goal, without providing support for this claim other than arguing that it is the source of our rational nature.

Korsgaard concludes from this that our actions towards animals would need to change quite radically, including the cessation of hunting, cruel experimentation, and the eating of animals. But this is after claiming that both plants and animals are similar in that they are both "self-maintaining beings and in that sense are oriented toward their own good" (2005, p. 106). She has not fully established a clear line between plants and animals, in terms of moral obligations, and yet she supports a clear line between rational and animal nature. In the end, her suggestions for how we ought to act towards animals sounds very much like Kant's own view on indirect duties (with the exception of not eating animals).

In a later work, Korsgaard (2011) does consider the different kinds of self-consciousness in animals and humans, in an attempt to clarify the key differences between them, and explain why animals ultimately do not have a rational nature. She acknowledges that animals have some forms of self-consciousness, in their abilities to be aware of themselves in space, and sometimes in their abilities to be aware of their own emotions and desires. She does not deny that animals possess various levels of intelligence that allow them to direct their own behaviours in accordance with their desires and goals. But she denies that animals are aware of their reasons for acting, and argues that animals cannot provide justifications of their actions by reflecting on their reasons. This is a result of her view of reason itself, and what it means to be rational, as opposed to what it means to be intelligent. Korsgaard explains this, saying:

> Reason looks inward, and focuses on the connections between our own mental states and attitudes and the effects that they tend to have on us. It asks whether our actions are justified by our motives or our inferences are justified by our beliefs. I think we could say things about the beliefs of

intelligent non-human animals that parallel what I have said about their actions. Non-human animals may have beliefs and may arrive at those beliefs under the influence of evidence; by analogy with our own case we may say that they have reasons for their beliefs. But it is a further step to be the sort of animal who can ask yourself whether the evidence really justifies the belief, and can adjust your conclusions accordingly…Human beings have a particular form or type of self-consciousness: consciousness of the grounds of our beliefs and actions. (2011, pp. 92–93)

She claims that this makes a big difference to the kind of self-consciousness between animals and humans, in that for humans, this allows for normative self-government, which she believes is the essence of morality and autonomy. This means that humans are rational and autonomous, whereas animals are not. Animals are thus moral patients rather than moral agents, and this means that only humans can will universal moral laws regarding our obligations towards them, wheraas animals cannot.

What this means for her argument is that although she has recognized that some animals are self-conscious in some ways, it still does not grant them autonomy or agency. She maintains the distinction between animal and rational nature and maintains that our obligations are based on what we have in common with animal nature. Humans have a rational, autonomous self, and an animal self. We can confer value as lawmakers on our own animal natures, and on the animal self found in non-human animals. It is by virtue of the natural goods that result from our animal natures that we are the kinds of rational creatures that can will moral laws into existence, and which obligate us towards each other and towards other animals. However, due to the ambiguities of natural goods, and without granting animals autonomy, the problem remains of how we can have direct moral obligations towards animals themselves if the value they have is dependent on our willing it, and if animal nature is only valuable as a means to rational nature. This may explain why her view, which she claims would radically alter the ways we treat animals, ends up sounding so similar to Kant's view on our indirect duties regarding animals, as I posited earlier.

Although Korsgaard makes reference to some research on the mental capacities of animals in her later work, she dismisses the possibility that this research demonstrates rationality. In dismissing the importance of research into animal minds and their cognitive abilities as irrelevant to her own argument, Korsgaard is maintaining a clear distinction between rational and non-rational nature. Extensive research shows however, that this line is not so easy to maintain, given the ability of many mammals to direct their own actions towards their goals, their abilities to communicate and learn language, and so on. If reason is a feature of consciousness, then certainly there are degrees of it that correlate to the various levels of consciousness, agency, and self-awareness. Animals with more reasons for acting can be considered more rational than those who have fewer reasons for acting, but both should be considered rational. Animals who are agents will be able to direct their actions towards their own goals to varying degrees, and the extent to which they have control over their behaviours will also indicate their level of autonomy. In a practical attempt to treat animals according to their nature, we must learn about their capacities through this sort of research. And this research is not irrelevant to establishing an argument in favour of direct moral obligations towards animals, as it helps us determine the extent to which we owe animals obligations based on their degree of selfhood and corresponding degree of autonomy. If animals possess even minimal selfhood and are minimally autonomous, then it is not us, as humans, who are placing value on them. Rather, it is by virtue of their agency, selfhood, and autonomy, and the importance of those features as determinants of moral value that obligate us towards them.

If we accept Korsgaard's line of reasoning, and posit the view that animals do not have the same kind of self-concept that humans do, we are unable to achieve the level of normative restrictions on our treatment of animals that she claims. This brings us back to the idea of what it means to be an entity that has a good. If plants and animals both have natural goods, and the only difference between them is some sort of deeper sense in which animals are aware of their own goods, it is difficult to see how we can achieve the level of difference in the way we ought to treat animals as opposed to plants. It seems that there is an important difference between the way in which plants have goods and the way in which animals have goods. If that is true, then it would seem that we also need to legislate for duties towards plants, including things like the cessation of harvesting plants for food, growing plants for experiments with toxic chemicals, and the picking of flowers for our kitchen centerpieces.

What I am arguing is that if animal nature is basically a consideration of natural goods in living entities, and a self-concept is not required for direct moral consideration, then it is not clear how we are to distinguish between the importance of those natural goods for plants and animals. If we are to be primarily concerned with natural goods, then are we not obligated to protect them in all living entities, as we share with them the desire to have our goods met and not interfered with—including plants?

Korsgaard argues that animals have goods in a *deeper* sense than plants as they experience the attainment of their needs, and that these experiences are the bases of their incentives, with their own good as the goal of their actions. What is significantly different here from the account we have of plants? The difference seems to reside in the ability of animals to experience and pursue their natural goods, whereas plants do not. The questions that can now be asked are, what is the nature of this experience for the animal, and what allows the animal to pursue various means to achieve its goal? I think this is where the importance of a selfhood enters the picture. An animal that can experience the satisfaction of its needs, and pursue the sorts of actions required to fulfil those needs requires at minimum, a certain level of consciousness.

I would argue further that, more specifically, it requires at least minimal self-awareness. If animals are conscious (particularly self-conscious) and plants are not, then it would seem that we are discussing a difference in kind, and not only of degree, in terms of a living entity that has natural goods for itself. Besides, the kind of good that Korsgaard ascribes to plants is not the kind of good that would obligate us towards them directly. If animals have the same kind of good as plants, then we would not be directly obligated towards them either. The difference between the two lies directly in the self that animals possess and that plants do not. Animal nature, as Korsgaard describes it, does not seem valuable only in its status as a precursor to rational nature, but rather it is valuable in its own right. An animal can direct its actions towards the fulfilment of its goods, and can also experience the fulfilment of these goods as pleasurable. It can do these things because it is self-aware and an agent.

I believe that for an animal to experience the fulfilment of its own goods as pleasurable, it must also have the capacity, even minimally, to evaluate those fulfilments, and to associate them with itself. An animal that can touch the painted dot on her forehead while looking at herself in a mirror does know, at least minimally, that the dot she is touching is on her body, and not someone else's. An animal that responds to the sound of his name being called knows, at least minimally, that that sound relates to him, and not some other animal. But how does this all relate back to the necessity of a self-concept for direct moral duties? When Korsgaard argues that the only requirement for direct duties to animals lies in the shared animal nature between human and non-humans, she is basing this on the idea that we share the same kinds of natural goods, and that we both experience the fulfilment of those natural goods in the same ways. And yet, she is not willing to concede that humans and non-human animals share a rational nature, but rather that rational nature is grounded in and emerges from animal nature. It seems to me that we cannot gain direct moral duties to animals, based on the notion that natural goods for a creature that matters to itself is also applicable to plants.

A self-concept in animals would make more sense of the idea that animals matter to themselves in a deeper sense than plants matter to themselves, as Korsgaard suggests. But from this I would argue that what Korsgaard is really talking about is the existence of at least a minimally rational nature in animals, or at least some animals. A full account of what kind of evidence we can find for associating reason with animals cannot be provided here, but it seems that accepting Korsgaard's conclusions about the kinds of changes required in our treatment of animals, also requires the acceptance of a minimally rational animal nature. Korsgaard would not be able to accept this conclusion and at the same time maintain the distinction in kind between rational human nature and non-human animal nature. Any duties towards animals would need to be based on duties to animals that do not result solely from our legislation of them, as rational agents, but rather from the idea that Kant was wrong about the nature of animals themselves.

Wright, Wood, and Korsgaard could all develop their views further by considering the body of evidence we have to support the idea that animals are intentional agents who are self-aware and autonomous. Without this support, it makes it difficult to argue that animals should be understood as lacking rational nature or autonomy, in terms of the ability to act for reasons. It would also benefit their views to consider more thoroughly how the actual treatment of animals would change, given the arguments they have presented in favour of treating animals as ends in themselves. This is certainly a large task, but one worth performing as it can bring to light the importance of specific mental capacities in our treatment of different individual animals and species. For example, the extent to which an animal possesses fragments of a rational nature, and which fragments they possess, for Wood, would surely result in different levels of moral consideration for individual animals. Similarly, for Wright, the more complex the mental capacities an animal has, the greater number of choices they can identify in their environments and particular contexts, and so those with more available choices for action would be owed greater moral consideration, as they also possess the ability to act freely in a larger sense. In these ways, the inclusion of research into animal minds and their mental capacities would strengthen post-Kantian views on animals.

Conclusion

Kantian ethics provides a strong foundation for valuing autonomy and selfhood in humans, as well as indirect duties regarding animals. However, in order to reinterpret Kant's arguments to provide support for direct moral duties towards animals, an argument must be made to include animals in the category of ends in themselves. Wright, Wood, and Korsgaard provide strong arguments in favour of doing so, even though their views have weaknesses, which I have explained in this chapter. For them, the ability of an individual to choose an end to pursue is what grants animals direct moral consideration. For Wright, the ability to choose redefines rational nature itself in his negative freedom view, and in this way we can consider animals as ends in themselves. For Korsgaard, this feature results from our shared animal nature, as creatures for whom ends matter, which includes both humans and other animals. For Wood, we ought to respect rational nature in the abstract, which means respecting animals by virtue of the fragments of rationality they possess. While Korsgaard maintains that animals are not autonomous or rational, Wright considers animals minimally autonomous due to their ability to make choices. Wood's view also seems to imply that animals can be minimally autonomous, but he is not explicit on this point, and he does not base the moral consideration of animals on it. My own view, which focuses on the moral value of selfhood and respect for autonomy, provides some ways to address the problems faced by these post-Kantian views, by taking into account the research and arguments which show that animals possess mental capacities that should provide them access to Kant's kingdom of ends.

References

Druce, Clare and Philip Lymbery. (2006). Outlawed in Europe. In Peter Singer (Ed.), *In Defense of Animals: The Second Wave* (pp. 123–131). Malden: Blackwell Publishers.
Kant, I. (1963). *Lectures on ethics* (L. Infield, Trans.). New York: Harper Torchbooks.
Kant, I. (1964). *Groundwork of the metaphysics of morals* (H. J. Paton, Trans.). Toronto: Harper Torchbooks.
Kant, I. (1991). *The metaphysics of morals* (M. Gregor, Trans.). New York: Cambridge University Press.
Korsgaard, C. (2005). *Fellow creatures: Kantian ethics and our duties to animals.* The Tanner Lectures on Human Values, University of Michigan. Retrieved November 5, 2006, from http://www.tannerlectures.utah.edu/lectures/documents/volume25/korsgaard_2005.pdf
Korsgaard, C. (2006). Morality and the distinctiveness of human action. In F. de Waal (Ed.), *Primates and philosophers: How morality evolved* (pp. 98–119). Princeton: Princeton University Press.
Korsgaard, C. (2011). Interacting with animals: A Kantian account. In T. Beauchamp & R. G. Frey (Eds.), *The Oxford handbook of animal ethics* (pp. 91–118). New York: Oxford University Press.
Korsgaard, C. (2012). A Kantian case for animal rights. In J. Hanni, M. Michel, & D. Kuhne. *Animal law: Tier und Recht* (pp. 1–28). Zurich, Dike Verlag.
Moral Self-Regard: Duties to Oneself in Kant's Moral Theory. Studies in Philosophy. New York: Garland, 2001.
Skidmore, J. (2001). Duties to animals: The failure of Kant's moral theory. *The Journal of Value Inquiry, 35*, 541–559.
Wood, A. W. (1998). Kant on duties regarding nonrational nature. *Proceedings of the Aristotelian Society, Supplementary Volume, 72*(1), 189–210.
Wright, William A. (1993). Treating animals as ends. The Journal of Value Inquiry, 27, 353–366.

7

Conclusions and Further Directions

Many animals, including mammals and some birds, are minimal, self-aware agents, and autonomous beings that are deserving of direct moral consideration. As research into animal minds continues, we will gain more understanding of the specific mental capacities that constitute selfhood, and this can be used to better gauge the particular ways we can respect autonomy in various individuals and species. Although challenges exist in interpreting animal behaviours correctly to make inferences about the animals' experiences, too much scepticism that results in the denial of animal selfhood is unwarranted. An empirically informed theory of animal ethics is the best way to support the inclusion of animals in the moral community. In this book, I have argued for a view of agency and selfhood that is more or less complex, depending on the mental capacities for rationality and intentionality found within individual animals and species. I supported this view with evidence from scientific research into animal minds, and also with arguments based on the evolutionary continuity of animal species. I further argued that, based on animal agency and self-awareness, most animals are also autonomous, and that provides us with reasons to respect an individual's ability to value their subjective experiences and control their own behaviour. A view which holds that animals and humans are divided into separate moral categories cannot be maintained given my view of selfhood and autonomy as existing on an evolutionary continuum.

Many animal ethicists have argued that animals are morally considerable, but, as I have claimed, their theories lack an account of what makes all animals (human or nonhuman) fundamentally morally relevant, as they have failed to focus on the significance of agency, selfhood, and autonomy as those things that give rise to interests that matter to every self-aware individual. Singer, Regan, and Rollin have provided accounts of animal ethics that have had important impacts on animal welfare and rights, but the implications are that they are inadequate in overcoming the perceived divide between the moral value of humans and animals. For Singer, animals retain their status as resources for human use, as they lack autonomy and self-awareness. In Regan's account, the implications of both his high-level category of experiencing subjects-of-a-life and his abolitionist views result in a limited inclusion of animals in the moral community, and a problematic prohibition on human-animal relationships. Rollin provides more specific ways of respecting animals by virtue of their telos, but the problems inherent in such an ambiguous concept make his view challenging in practice, and can result in overlooking other individual characteristics that might be morally relevant to an animal's treatment. Gruen's account of entangled empathy provides support for valuing individual animals within the context of our relationships with them, but in denying the importance of establishing that animals are self-aware and autonomous, her view is limited in convincing others why they ought to care about animals with whom they do not have a personal relationship.

In my account, as agency, selfhood, and autonomy can exist in varying degrees, we are morally obligated towards animals to the extent that we can plausibly identify the complexity of an individual's agency and self-awareness, and this applies to all animals, including humans. As Wise (2000) shows, this can be practically implemented using an autonomy scale to classify animals and the duties we owe them according to the level of autonomy they possess. This shows the important role scientific research plays in developing an adequate ethic for animals, as it provides us with the information necessary to perform such a classification of moral obligations. It also means that autonomy is not just a human feature, although I have argued that there is no reason to give up a richer sense of autonomy, such as Frey's (1987) autonomy as control view, as long as we recognize that autonomy as choice is also deserving of moral respect.

I expanded this argument of minimal autonomy, or autonomy as choice, in conjunction with Kantian arguments that posit animals are ends in themselves. Although Wright, Wood, and Korsgaard make strong arguments in favour of this claim, they neglect the importance of selfhood, as a feature of consciousness, in making animal choices possible at all. While Wright seems to support my notion of autonomy in degrees, Korsgaard maintains the view that autonomy is only possible in fully reflective, rational agents. However, by arguing that animals can be minimally autonomous, I claimed that animals are deserving of respect and direct moral consideration as ends in themselves, and that Wright, Wood, and Korsgaard, if they acknowledged the evidence in support of selfhood in animals, would have stronger reasons to accept this claim. Rational autonomy, as the grounds for direct moral consideration on Kantian views, seems to admit to existing in degrees, in the same way as self-awareness and agency.

One important consideration to be made, in any theory of animal ethics, is where to draw the line, in terms of which individual animals or species are deserving of direct moral obligations. This is a difficult, if not impossible, question to answer. On the one hand, I think it sometimes serves to distract or prevent us from acting on obligations we have towards those animals that we know, with some degree of certainty, deserve this kind of direct moral consideration. For example, in debating whether or not fish are sentient, or capable of experiencing pain or suffering, it can be easier to discount the arguments in favour of fish having these capacities due to the fact that the debate even exists. We are more certain that pigs have the requisite mental capacities for the ability to suffer or experience pleasure so there is less debate about our knowledge in this area and we are more likely to consider them morally relevant than we are fish. One way to address this is to err on the side of caution, as I argued earlier, to ensure that in cases where we only have a limited amount of evidence to support claims that certain animals are self-aware, we ought to give them direct moral consideration. Vegans, for example, resist drawing the line by abiding by a hard and fast rule to not consume animal products of any kind, just in case species like bees, for example, are capable of suffering. Another way to address this issue is to ask more questions about the animal or species under debate, and carry out research to find out just what we do know about their mental capacities. We can ask, for example, if the species has any of the mental capacities that are indicators of self-awareness, or if there are anecdotal accounts of interactions with animals within that species that indicate agency or intentionality. We can then judge, based on this information, whether or not an animal or species should be considered self-aware and autonomous, and to what extent. Although all of these suggestions require time and effort, they provide ways for people to work through where to draw the line, based on reasons that can be evaluated and justified, rather than on arbitrary or inconsistent ones.

One other interesting, and increasingly pressing, consideration is the extent to which we owe species, as a whole, direct moral obligations. Although in this book I have examined animals as both individuals and species, I have not addressed the question of whether or not species themselves can be considered autonomous, or what should be done in cases where moral obligations towards individuals and species might conflict. Considering the moral value of a species is increasingly urgent as we face mass extinction events, and because we are also capable of genetically manipulating species in ways that previously were not possible. Ronald L. Sandler (2012) considers this topic and writes, "It is because we have the power to cause mass extinctions, substantially modify existing species, and create novel species that we require an ethic of species. Central to an ethic of species are an account of the value of species and an account of the ethical significance of species boundaries." (3). In his book he examines different ways we might ascribe moral value to species, and although he argues that all naturally evolved living species have inherent worth, our treatment of various animal species is, in part, dependent on the mental capacities that they possess. While it seems inaccurate to speak of a species itself as autonomous, the idea that its members are autonomous raises the question of how we can justify, for example, culling the members of a particular species to protect the integrity of another.

7 Conclusions and Further Directions

If the members of each species possess self-awareness and ought to be considered autonomous, then is it morally justifiable to infringe on that autonomy for the sake of the whole species, or for the sake of a different species? Although we also face conflicts when attempting to respect the autonomy of different human individuals or groups, it does not seem to be of the same magnitude when the potential consequences are the extinctions of entire species. The best attempt at an answer that I can provide here is to say that we would have to evaluate each species under consideration more carefully, both in terms of the mental capacities possessed by its members, and the extent to which its members are self-aware and autonomous. This would help to guide us in determining how we ought to treat the members of that species. The value of non-sentient species, like plants or bacteria, would clearly require a different source of value and moral consideration. These issues require more attention than can be provided here, but they are urgent areas for further examination.

Lastly, if we include selfhood and autonomy in the discussion about whether or not animals should be included in the moral community we have created as humans, then we cannot ignore the inconsistencies in our current treatment of animals. To do so would be arbitrary and irrational. Although animal welfare and animal rights proponents have made significant improvements for the well-being of animals, my view provides a middle path between the two that places an emphasis not only on the moral importance of the interests of animals, but also on animals themselves, and the relationships between animals, both human and non-human. The question that remains is why, if animals are self-aware, and if they possess similar mental capacities to those of humans, we continue to treat only certain kinds of animals with direct moral consideration?

I believe that the answer to this question is that there are various ways that humans have made animals and their subjectivity invisible. Through both visual and textual discourses, we represent animals as objects or things that are dissimilar to us, so that we can continue to use them for our own purposes without recognizing that they are self-aware and morally considerable individuals. And so here I will consider a few ways that we can make animal selves more visible.

One such way is to provide more accounts of the mental and emotional lives of animals, and to accept that anecdotal evidence of the selfhood in animals should be included in the body of evidence to support the claim that animals are, in fact, self-aware individuals. Writers and scientists like Marc Bekoff and Jane Goodall are examples of those who do this. By providing accounts of interactions with animals that people generally don't have access to, it offers information and knowledge about the rich mental and emotional lives of animals that is based on experience rather than relying on representations of animals in other media that may be neither accurate nor factual. Including in such accounts interactions with animals other than those with exotic, wild species, such as farm animals, can help to break down some of the arbitrary distinctions that are made between species that matter morally and those that do not.

Another related way that we can make animal selfhood more visible is by challenging their representations in the media. In both visual and textual representations of animals in the media, including those found in film, advertising, the news, and television, we are presented with the idea that animals are only valuable to the extent that we allow them to be. Often, animals are also reduced to the status of objects or things that exist solely for our own purposes, as evidenced by how we make real animals absent from the items we consume that are made from their body parts. The concept of the *absent referent* explains how this works through the use of language. Carol J. Adams (2015) explains this concept saying:

> Through butchering, animals become absent referents. Animals in name and body are made absent as animals for meat to exist. Animals' lives precede and enable the existence of meat. If animals are alive they cannot be meat. Thus a dead body replaces the live animal. Without animals there would be no meat eating, yet they are absent from the act of eating meat because they have been transformed into food. (20–21)

By making animals absent referents, we are making their individual selves invisible. In so doing, it enables us to keep meat separate from the real animal it came from, and it perpetuates the use of animals merely as a means to our own ends. The reality of the suffering that animals endure in farming practices is morally relevant as it belongs to self-aware individuals whose ability to act freely and make choices has been removed. But if we are able to ignore that the suffering we know exists belongs to actual, self-aware individuals, then there is no motivation to change our actions in terms of things like eating animal products.

We also need to identify and challenge the discourses that are embedded in the media and our culture that keep the subjectivity of animals invisible. This is because such discourses shape our understanding of animals in ways that seem normal and natural, but that are actually inaccurate. Discourses can create and reinforce relationships that thrive on the oppression of one by the other, by representing the less powerful group as undeserving of moral consideration. As Machin and Mayr (2012) claim, "Since language can [re]produce social life, what kind of world is being created by texts and what kinds of inequalities and interests might this seek to perpetuate, generate or legitimate? Here language is not simply a vehicle of communication, or for persuasion, but a means of social construction and domination." (24) Critical discourse analysis can be helpful in identifying and analyzing the ways that language works to create and affect our perceptions of animals, both by how animals are represented in discourses, and by how they are left out. Animal selfhood may be part of a scientific and philosophical discourse on animals, but in popular forms of discourse the subject is sorely lacking. Claire Molloy (2011) is correct when she says that, "where animals are not discursively constructed as having any moral worth, they are treated accordingly as property, objects, machines and things" (9). By not including animal selfhood as part of the popular discourse on animals, they are represented instead as objects for use in experimentation and research, or as pets to be bred, bought and sold, or as agricultural animals to be eaten. In all these ways, animals are represented as only having value insofar as they are commodities, and thus are denied direct moral consideration. And so, further consideration is needed of how we can make self-aware, autonomous animals visible in our discourses about them if we are to act on the moral obligations we have towards them.

References

Adams, C. J. (2015). *The sexual politics of meat: A feminist-vegetarian critical theory*. New York: Bloomsbury.
David Machin and Andrea Mayr 2012. How to Do Critical Discourse Analysis. A Multimodal Introduction. London: Sage.
Frey, R. G. (1987). Autonomy and the value of animal life. *The Monist, 70,* 50–63.
Machin, David and Andrea Mayr. (2013). *How To Do Critical Discourse Analysis: A Multimodal Introduction*. Thousand Oaks: SAGE Publications.
Molloy, C. (2011). *Popular media and animals*. Basingstoke: Palgrave Macmillan.
Sandler, R. L. (2012). *The ethics of species: An introduction*. New York: Cambridge University Press.
Wise, S. M. (2000). *Rattling the cage: Towards legal rights for animals*. Cambridge: Perseus Publishing.

Bibliography

Acampora, R. R. (2006). *Corporal compassion: Animal ethics and philosophy of body*. Pittsburgh: University of Pittsburgh Press.
Aguilar, J. H., Buckareff, A. A., & Frankish, K. (Eds.) (2011). *New waves in philosophy of action*. Basingstoke: Palgrave Macmillan.
Allen, C. (1998). The discovery of animal consciousness: An optimistic assessment. *Journal of Agricultural and Environmental Ethics, 10*, 217–225.
Allen, Colin, "Animal Consciousness", The Stanford Encyclopedia of Philosophy (Winter 2011 Edition), Edward N. Zalta (ed.), http://plato.stanford.edu/archives/win2011/entries/consciousnessanimal.
Armstrong, S. J., & Botzler, R. G. (2008). *The animal ethics reader* (2nd ed.). New York: Routledge.
Baker, L. R. (2000). *Persons and bodies: A constitution view*. New York: Cambridge University Press.
Barth, J., Reaux, J.E., & Povinelli, D.J. (2005). Chimpanzees' (Pan troglodytes) use of gaze cues in object-choice tasks: different methods yield different results. Animal Cognition, 8, 84–92.
Bekoff, Marc and Paul W. Sherman. (2004). Reflections on animal selves. Trends in Ecology and Evolution. Vol. 19, No. 4, 176–180
Bekoff, M., & Pierce, J. (2009). *Wild justice: The moral lives of animals*. Chicago: The University of Chicago Press.

Bermudez, J. L. (2003). *Thinking without words*. New York: Oxford University Press.
Bermudez, J. L. (2007). Thinking without words: An overview for animal ethics. *The Journal of Ethics, 11*, 319–335.
Brook, A., & DeVidi, R. C. (Eds.) (2001). *Self-reference and self-awareness*. Philadelphia: John Benjamins Publishing Company.
Budiansky, S. (1998). *If a lion could talk: Animal intelligence and the evolution of consciousness*. Toronto: The Free Press.
Buss, S., & Lee, O. (Eds.) (2002). *Contours of agency: Essays on themes from Harry Frankfurt*. Cambridge: The MIT Press.
Call, J., & Tomasello, M. (2005). Reasoning and thinking in nonhuman primates. In K. J. Holyoak & R. G. Morrison (Eds.), *The Cambridge handbook of thinking and reasoning* (pp. 607–632). New York: Cambridge University Press.
Carruthers, P. (2005a). Why the question of animal consciousness might not matter very much. *Philosophical Psychology, 18*(1), 83–102.
Carruthers, P. (2005b). Reply to Shriver and Allen. *Philosophical Psychology, 18*(1), 113–122.
Carruthers, P. (2005c). *Consciousness: Essays from a higher-order perspective*. Oxford: Clarendon Press.
Carruthers, P. (2007). Invertebrate minds: A challenge for ethical theory. *The Journal of Ethics, 11*, 275–297.
Cartmill, M. (2000). Animal consciousness: Some philosophical, methodological, and evolutionary problems. *American Zoologist, 40*(6), 835–836.
Cavalieri, P. (2009). *The death of the animal: A dialogue*. New York: Columbia University.
Chandroo, K. P., Duncan, I. J. H., & Moccia, R. D. (2004). Can fish suffer?: Perspectives on sentience, pain, fear and stress. *Applied Animal Behaviour Science, 86*, 225–250.
Christman, J. (Ed.) (1989). *The inner citadel: Essays on individual autonomy*. New York: Oxford University Press.
Clark, S. R. L. (1982). *The nature of the beast: Are animals moral?* New York: Oxford University Press.
Dawkins, M. S. (2000). Animal minds and animal emotions. *American Zoologist, 40*(6), 883–888.
DeGrazia, David. (2009). Self-awareness in animals. In Lurz, Robert W. (Ed.) The Philosophy of Animal Minds. New York: Cambridge University Press, 201–217.
Denis, L. (2001). *Moral self-regard: Duties to oneself in Kant's moral theory*. New York: Garland Publishers, Inc.
Dennett, D. C. (1987). *The intentional stance*. Cambridge: The MIT Press.

Dennett, D. C. (1996). *Kinds of minds: Towards an understanding of consciousness.* New York: BasicBooks.
Dennett, D. C. (1998). *Brainchildren: Essays on designing minds.* Cambridge: The MIT Press.
De Veer, M. W., Gallup Jr., G. G., Theall, L. A., van den Bos, R., & Povinelli, D. J. (2003). An 8-year longitudinal study of mirror self-recognition in chimpanzees. *Neuropsychologia, 41*, 229–234.
Dixon, B. A. (2008). *Animals: Emotion & morality: Marking the boundary.* New York: Prometheus Books.
Dol, M., Kasanmoentalib, S., Lijmbach, S., Rivas, E., & van den Bos, R. (Eds.) (1997). *Animal consciousness and animal ethics: Perspectives from the Netherlands.* Assen: Van Gorcum.
Domasio, A. (1999). *The feeling of what happens: Body and emotion in the making of consciousness.* New York: A Harvest Book, Harcourt Inc.
Domasio, A. (2010). *Self comes to mind: Constructing the conscious brain.* New York: Pantheon Books.
Dretske, F. I. (1999). Machines, plants and animals: The origins of agency. *Erkenntnis, 51*, 19–31.
Droege, P. (2012). Assessing evidence for animal consciousness: The question of episodic memory. In J. A. Smith & R. W. Mitchell (Eds.), *Experiencing animal minds: An anthology of animal-human encounters* (pp. 231–245). New York: Columbia University Press.
Druce, Clare and Philip Lymbery. (2006). Outlawed in Europe. In Peter Singer (Ed.), In Defense of Animals: The Second Wave (pp. 123–131). Malden: Blackwell Publishers.
Fellenz, M. R. (2007). *The moral menagerie: Philosophy and animal rights.* Urbana: University of Illinois Press.
Ferrari, M., & Sternberg, R. J. (1998). *Self-awareness: Its nature and development.* New York: The Guilford Press.
Flanagan, O. (2007). *The really hard problem: Meaning in a material world.* Cambridge: The MIT Press.
Foot, P. (1978). *Virtues and vices and other essays in moral philosophy.* Berkeley: University of California Press.
Foot, P. (2001). *Natural goodness.* Toronto: Oxford University Press.
Francescotti, R. (2007). Animal mind and animal ethics: An introduction. *The Journal of Ethics, 11*, 239–252.
Francione, G. L. (1996). *Rain without thunder: The ideology of the animal rights movement.* Philadelphia: Temple University Press.
Frankfurt, H. G. (1971). Freedom of the will and the concept of a person. *The Journal of Philosophy, 68*(1), 5–20.

Genarro, R. J. (2004). Higher-order thoughts, animal consciousness, and misrepresentation: A reply to Carruthers and Levine. In R. J. Genarro (Ed.), *Higher order theories of consciousness: An anthology* (pp. 45–66). Philadelphia: John Benjamins North America.

Gewirth, A. (1998). *Self-fulfillment*. Princeton: Princeton University Press.

Gilhus, I. S. (2006). *Animals, gods and humans: Changing attitudes to animals in Greek, Roman and early Christian ideas*. New York: Routledge.

Griffin, D. R. (1981). *The question of animal awareness: Evolutionary continuity of mental experience*. New York: The Rockefeller University Press.

Griffin, D. R. (2000). Scientific approaches to animal consciousness. *American Zoologist, 40*(6), 889–892.

Hare, R. M. (1981). *Moral thinking: Its levels, method, and point*. Oxford: Clarendon Press.

Hauser, M. D. (2006). *Moral minds: The nature of right and wrong*. Toronto: Harper Perennial.

Haworth, L. (1986). *Autonomy: An essay in philosophical psychology and ethics*. New Haven: Yale University Press.

Huebner, B. (2011). Minimal minds. In T. L. Beauchamp & R. G. Frey (Eds.), *The Oxford handbook of animal ethics* (pp. 1–21). Oxford University Press.

Hurley, S. L. (1998). *Consciousness in action*. Cambridge: Harvard University Press.

Hurley, S., & Nudds, M. (2006). *Rational animals?* New York: Oxford University Press.

Hursthouse, R. (2000). *Ethics, humans and other animals: An introduction with readings*. New York: Routledge.

Kemmerer, L. (2006). *In search of consistency: Ethics and animals*. Boston: Brill.

Kheel, M. (2008). *Nature ethics: An ecofeminist perspective*. Toronto: Rowman & Littlefield Publishers, Inc.

Kistler, J. M. (2000). *Animal rights: A subject guide, bibliography, and Internet companion*. Westport: Greenwood Press.

Kolak, D., & Martin, R. (Eds.) (1991). *Self and identity: Contemporary philosophical issues*. Toronto: Collier Macmillan Canada.

Langford, D. J., Crager, S. E., Shehzad, Z., Smith, S. B., Sotocinal, S. G., Levenstadt, J. S., et al. (2006). Social modulation of pain as evidence of empathy in mice. *Science, 312*(5782), 1967–1970.

Leary, M. R., & Buttermore, N. R. (2003). The evolution of the human self: Tracing the natural history of self-awareness. *Journal for the Theory of Social Behaviour, 33*(4), 365–404.

Lehman, H. (1998). Animal awareness. *Applied Animal Behaviour Science, 57*, 315–325.

Linzey, A., & Clarke, P. B. (Eds.) (2004). *Animal rights: A historical anthology*. New York: Columbia University Press.

Lurz, R. W. (Ed.) (2009). *The philosophy of animal minds*. New York: Cambridge University Press.

Lurz, R. W. (2011). *Mindreading animals: The debate over what animals know about other minds*. Cambridge: The MIT Press.

Machin, D., & Mayr, A. (2013). *How to do critical discourse analysis: A multimodal introduction*. Thousand Oaks: SAGE Publications.

Malle, B. F., & Hodges, S. D. (Eds.) (2005). *Other minds: How humans bridge the divide between self and others*. New York: The Guilford Press.

Martin, R., & Barresi, J. (Eds.) (2003). *Personal identity*. Malden: Blackwell Publishing.

Mazis, G. A. (2008). *Humans, animals, machines: Blurring boundaries*. New York: Suny Press.

Mele, A. R. (1995). *Autonomous agents: From self-control to autonomy*. New York: Oxford University Press.

Mensch, J. R. (2003). *Ethics and selfhood: Alterity and the phenomenology of obligation*. New York: State University of New York Press.

Midgley, M. (1983). *Animals and why they matter*. Athens: The University of Georgia Press.

Miller, H. B., & Williams, W. H. (Eds.) (1983). *Ethics and animals*. Clifton: Humana Press.

Milligan, T. (2015). *Animal ethics: The basics*. New York: Routledge.

Mitchell, R. W. (1997). Kinesthetic-visual matching and the self-concept as explanations of mirror-self-recognition. *Journal for the Theory of Social Behaviour, 27*(1), 17–39.

Morin, A. (2006). Levels of consciousness and self-awareness: A comparison and integration of various views. *Consciousness and Cognition, 15*(2), 358–371.

Munro, L. (2005). *Confronting animal cruelty: Moral orthodoxy and the challenge of the animal rights movement*. Boston: Brill.

Nagel, T. (1986). *The view from nowhere*. New York: Oxford University Press.

Nagel, T. (1995). *Other minds: Critical essays 1969–1994*. New York: Cambridge University Press.

Newmyer, S. T. (2006). *Animals, rights and reason in Plutarch and modern ethics*. New York: Routledge.

Noske, B. (1997). *Beyond boundaries: Humans and animals*. Montreal: Black Rose Books.

Palmer, C. (2010). *Animal ethics in context*. New York: Columbia University Press.

Parker, S. T., Mitchell, R. W., & Boccia, M. L. (Eds.) (1994). *Self-awareness in animals and humans: Developmental perspectives*. New York: Cambridge University Press.

Peterson, G. R. (2003). Being conscious of Marc Bekoff: Thinking of animal self-consciousness. *Zygon, 38*(2), 247–256.
Petrus, K., & Wild, M. (Eds.) (2013). *Animal minds & animal ethics: Connecting two separate fields.* Bielefeld: transcript Verlag.
Piggins, D., & Phillips, C. J. C. (1998). Awareness in domesticated animals—Concepts and definitions. *Applied Animal Behaviour Sciences, 57,* 181–200.
Povinelli, D. J., & Vonk, J. (2003). Chimpanzee minds: Suspiciously human? *Trends in Cognitive Sciences, 7*(4), 157–160.
Povinelli, D. J., & Vonk, J. (2004). We don't need a microscope to explore the chimpanzee's mind. *Mind and Language, 19*(1), 1–28.
Reath, A. (2006). *Agency and autonomy in Kant's moral theory.* Oxford: Clarendon Press.
Regan, T. (2003). *Animal rights, human wrongs: An introduction to moral philosophy.* Toronto: Rowman & Littlefield.
Robinson, D. N. (2008). *Consciousness and mental life.* New York: Columbia University Press.
Rochat, P. (2003). Five levels of self-awareness as they unfold early in life. *Consciousness and Cognition, 12,* 717–731.
Roessler, J., & Eilan, N. (Eds.) (2003). *Agency and self-awareness: Issues in philosophy and psychology.* Toronto: Oxford University Press.
Rollin, B. E. (1989). *The unheeded cry: Animal consciousness, animal pain, and science.* Toronto: Oxford University Press.
Rollin, B. E. (2007). Animal mind: Science, philosophy, and ethics. *The Journal of Ethics, 11,* 253–274.
Rowlands, M. (2002). *Animals like us.* New York: Verso.
Russon, A. E., Bard, K. A., & Parker, S. T. (Eds.) (1996). *Reaching into thought: The minds of the great apes.* New York: Cambridge University Press.
Savage-Rumbaugh, S., Fields, W. M., & Tagliatela, J. (2000). Ape consciousness—Human consciousness: A perspective informed by language and culture. *American Zoologist, 40*(6), 910–921.
Schilhab, T. S. S. (2004). What mirror self-recognition in nonhumans can tell us about aspects of self. *Biology and Philosophy, 19,* 111–126.
Scully, M. (2002). *Dominion: The power of man, the suffering of animals, and the call to mercy.* New York: St. Martin's Press.
Seyfarth, R. M., & Cheney, D. L. (2000). Social awareness in monkeys. *American Zoologist, 40*(6), 902–909.
Shriver, A., & Allen, C. (2005). Consciousness might matter very much. *Philosophical Psychology, 18*(1), 103–111.

Singer, P. (1975). *Animal liberation: A new ethics for our treatment of animals*. New York: Avon Books.
Singer, P. (Ed.) (1985). *In defense of animals*. New York: Basil Blackwell.
Singer, P. (Ed.) (2006). *In defense of animals: The second wave*. Malden: Blackwell Publishers.
Smith, J. A., & Mitchell, R. W. (Eds.) (2012). *Experiencing animal minds: An anthology of animal-human encounters*. New York: Columbia University Press.
Smuts, B. (2001). Encounters with animal minds. *Journal of Consciousness Studies, 8*(5-7), 293–309.
Sorabji, R. (1993). *Animal minds and human morals: The origins of the Western debate*. Ithaca: Cornell University Press.
Sorabji, R. (2006). *Self: Ancient and modern insights about individuality, life, and death*. Chicago: The University of Chicago Press.
Spiegel, M. (1996). *The dreaded comparison: Human and animal slavery*. New York: Mirror Books.
Steinbock, B. (1992). *Life before birth: The moral and legal status of embryos and fetuses*. New York: Oxford University Press.
Steiner, G. (2008). *Animals and the moral community: Mental life, moral status, and kinship*. New York: Columbia University Press.
Sunstein, C. R., & Nussbaum, M. C. (Eds.) (2004). *Animal rights: Current debates and new directions*. Toronto: Oxford University Press.
Taylor, A. (2009). *Animals & ethics: An overview of the philosophical debate* (3rd ed.). Peterborough: Broadview Press.
Terrace, H. S., & Metcalfe, J. (Eds.) (2005). *The missing link in cognition: Origins of self-reflective consciousness*. Toronto: Oxford University Press.
Thompson, E. (2007). *Mind in life: Biology, phenomenology, and the sciences of the mind*. Cambridge: The Belknap Press of Harvard University Press.
Turner, J., & D'Silva, J. (Eds.) (2006). *Animals, ethics and trade: The challenge of animal sentience*. Sterling: Earthscan.
Toda, Koji and Shigeru Watanabe. (2008). Discrimination of moving video images of self by pigeons (Columba livia). Animal Cognition, 11, 699–705
White, S. L. (1991). *The unity of the self*. Cambridge: The MIT Press.
Wilson, H. L. (2008). The green Kant: Kant's treatment of animals. In L. P. Pojman & P. Pojman (Eds.), *Environmental ethics: Readings in theory and application* (5th ed., pp. 65–72). Belmont: Thomson Higher Education.
Wright, William A. (1993). Treating animals as ends. The Journal of Value Inquiry, 27, 353–366.

Index

A
action
  consistency in, 2, 46, 83
  intentional, 9, 19, 20, 44, 58, 78, 81
Adams, Carol J., 160
agency
  biological, 8, 9, 22, 39, 86
  moral, 27–34, 73–5, 80, 139
  rational, 9, 87, 131
agents
  acting, 4, 5, 23, 27, 28, 32
  autonomous, 2, 29, 74, 84, 125, 126
  intentional, 3, 4, 10, 12, 13, 17, 18, 21, 23, 25, 35, 107, 140, 151
  marginal, 86
  minimal, 8
  prospective, 84, 85
  purposive, 84
  rational, 12, 131, 132, 138, 145, 151, 157
  self-aware, 5, 10, 94, 125, 155
Allen, Colin, 13
Andrews, Kristin, 8, 10, 16, 80
Angell, Tony, 64
animal
  abolitionists, 116
  as absent referent, 160
  altruism, 30, 31
  beliefs, 12, 13, 15, 92
  cognition, 8, 11
  communication, 50, 59, 60
  companion, 1, 3, 53, 80, 83, 86, 90, 93, 113, 123, 135, 137
  eating, 102, 103, 147
  emotions, 11

animal (cont.)
  empathy, 1, 5, 29–32, 40,
    119–26, 156
  experiences, 1, 2, 4, 9, 11, 34,
    38, 39, 41, 42, 44–7, 49,
    50, 52–4, 57, 58, 61, 62,
    64, 65, 69, 73, 82, 106,
    107, 121–5, 136, 142, 146,
    150, 155, 156
  gaze-following, 60
  goals, 5, 9, 19, 21, 22, 24, 25, 28,
    44, 61, 74, 75, 78, 79, 86,
    88, 107, 109, 135, 147, 149
  interests, 48
  killing, 47, 75, 76, 102, 132
  minds, 1, 3, 4, 6, 7, 11, 15,
    16, 26, 27, 42, 63, 65,
    84, 86, 114, 125, 137,
    149, 152, 155
  mirror self-recognition tests, 31,
    39, 61, 78, 146
  pain, 40, 41, 47, 51, 62, 79,
    85, 88, 89, 103, 105–7,
    115, 132, 139, 140, 142,
    144, 157
  play, 135
  problem-solving skills, 19, 58
  as rational agents, 151
  rights, 76, 113, 159
  sense of fairness, 29, 32
  social, 29–32, 35, 38, 40, 41, 45,
    47, 53, 59, 61, 79, 88–90,
    94, 107, 117, 122, 124,
    137, 146, 161
  species and variants, 6, 30, 40, 49,
    50, 79, 111, 155, 158
    ants, 41, 58
    bats, 42, 65, 93

beavers, 58
birds, 6, 7, 18, 32, 43, 57, 58,
  64, 107, 108, 112, 117–19,
  137, 155
blue jays, 58
cats, 1, 53, 54, 59, 123
cephalopods, 57
chickens, 102, 123, 135, 137
chimpanzees, 24, 41, 56, 57,
  60, 123
chipmunks, 123
corvids, 64
cows, 57, 113, 137
crabs, 58
crows, 41, 58, 64
cuttlefish, 57
Darwin's finches, 58
dogs, 1, 7, 53, 54, 60, 88, 90,
  93, 98, 114, 123
dolphins, 28, 29, 39, 56, 57,
  59, 60, 62, 89, 90, 98
Egyptian vultures, 58
elephants, 29, 39, 56, 58, 62
farm, 123, 137, 160
fish, 6, 43, 59, 107, 137, 157
goats, 59
gorillas, 57
great apes, 56, 82
mammals, 6, 32, 86, 107–9,
  112, 149, 155
marsh tit, 57
mice, 57, 87
octopus, 57
parrots, 60
pigs, 57, 58, 120, 123,
  137, 157
primates, 28, 29, 38, 59, 60,
  62, 91, 135, 137

rats, 24, 57
ravens, 58
rhesus monkeys, 41, 57
rodents, 57, 58
rooks, 58
scrub jays, 57
sea otters, 58
sheep, 59
squirrels, 12–14, 16
wasps, 58
whales, 65
wolf, 109
suffering, 3, 5, 34, 47, 62, 72, 75, 79, 88, 89, 99–105, 108, 125, 132, 157, 158, 160, 161
sympathy, 29, 31–4, 40
tool use, 4, 19, 58, 59
welfarists, 3, 113
anthropodenial, 26, 27
anthropomorphism, 25–7, 62–5, 92, 119
Aristotle, 73, 117
Arpaly, Nomy, 72
autonomy
  as alternatives, 87
  basic, 77, 88, 89
  common view of, 70–7, 87, 94
  as control, 76, 157
  Kantian, 105
  minimal, 70, 77–82, 136, 139, 157
  naturalized view of, 87–9
  practical, 77, 78
  preference, 76, 109, 139
  rich, 77, 88
  'umbrella view' of, 80

B
Bekoff, Marc, 11, 40, 160
beliefs, 2, 3, 8–17, 19–28, 30, 34, 35, 37, 39, 44, 54, 60, 61, 64, 71, 75, 80, 81, 83, 90–2, 107, 108, 137, 141, 146–8
Bentham, Jeremy, 99
Bickerton, Derek, 50, 51
Broom, Donald M., 57, 58
Butterworth, George, 52

C
Cavalieri, Paola, 105
Cheney, Dorothy L., 39, 61
children, 14, 17, 32, 39, 46, 56, 80–3, 110, 134, 138, 140, 141
Christman, John, 81
cognitivism, 10
concepts, in animals, 15
consciousness
  higher-order, 39, 74
  phenomenal, 42, 43, 65
  self-consciousness, 19, 38–49, 91, 135, 136, 146–8
continuity
  evolutionary, 29, 49–55, 63–5, 87, 135, 155
  species, 65

D
Dawkins, M. S., 38
DeGrazia, David, 44
Denis, Lara, 132

Dennett, Daniel C., 12, 20, 21, 25–7, 44
desires
 first-order, 74–6
 second-order, 74, 75
de Waal, Frans, 26
discourses, 151, 161
Dretske, Fred, 17, 18
Druce, Clare, 137
duties
 direct, 130, 131, 145, 151
 indirect, 130, 132, 147, 148, 152
 moral, 3, 32, 70, 71, 129–31, 138, 140, 147, 151, 152
Dworkin, Gerald, 71

empathy
 in animals, 1, 5, 29–32, 40, 119–26, 156
 entangled, 120–6, 156
ends-in-themselves, 6, 49
ethics
 of care, 121
 feminist, 121
 Kantian, 129–53
 relational, 97, 98, 121, 124
 utilitarian, 49, 98–108, 115, 116, 120, 125, 126, 133
ethology, cognitive, 39, 90

Francione, Gary, 113
Franklin, Julian H., 105, 110
Frey, R. G., 75, 76, 157

Gallup, Gordon G., 61, 62
Garner, Robert, 110
Genarro, Rocco J., 57
Gewirth, Alan, 83
Glock, Hans-Johann, 19
goal
 -*directed*, 23–5, 44
 -*oriented*, 23–5
Goodall, Jane, 160
Griffin, Donald R., 38, 50, 58, 59, 61, 63
Gruen, Lori, 5, 98, 120–5

homocentrism, 86

intentionality, 15, 20–7, 35, 44, 81, 82, 155, 158
intentional stance, 18, 20, 21, 25
interests
 animal, 48
 plant, 107, 112, 115, 144, 145, 159
 principle of equal consideration of, 99–101
internal mental states, 24
Irvine, Leslie, 53–5

justice, 83, 121

K

Kant, Immanuel, 130
Kaplan, Gisela, 59, 60, 79
Korsgaard, Christine, 80, 134

L

language, 13, 14, 16, 19, 21, 26, 27, 29, 44, 47, 51, 59, 60, 78, 81, 149, 160, 161
Linzey, Andrew, 92
Lymbery, Philip, 137

M

Machin, David, 161
machines, 21, 25, 161
Marino, Lori, 56
Martin, Kenneth, 56
Marzluff, John, 64
Mayr, Andrea, 161
McGinn, Colin, 45–7
memory
 in animals, 52, 54, 55, 57, 74, 101, 107, 108
 episodic, 57
metacognition, 28
Miller, Harlan B., 47–9
minds
 animal, 1, 2, 6, 7, 11, 15, 16, 26, 27, 42, 63, 65, 84, 86, 114, 125, 137, 149, 152, 155
 problem of other minds, 42
Molloy, Claire, 161
moral
 agents, 4, 28, 30, 32, 33, 35, 47, 73, 80, 86, 108, 115, 122, 132, 136, 140, 141, 144, 148
 obligations, 4–7, 10, 23, 47, 70, 71, 76, 77, 82, 83, 89, 94, 97, 98, 102, 106, 108, 110–12, 117, 119, 120, 130, 133–6, 139–42, 143, 144, 147–9, 157, 158, 161
 patients, 28, 108, 112, 136, 148
 status, 28, 77, 102, 131
 subjects, 28, 77, 102, 131
Morgan's Canon, 63
Morin, Alain, 44, 45

N

Nagel, Thomas, 42
nature
 animal, 130, 140–52
 rational, 130, 133, 134, 136, 138–40, 142–4, 146–9, 150–2
Neisser, Ulric, 52

O

O'Brien, Lilian, 9
Okrent, Mark, 21–3

P

paternalism, 80, 109
Pepperberg, Irene, 60
perception, 1, 42, 52, 107, 122
personhood, 71, 75, 102, 110
pets, 90, 135, 161
plants, 21, 23, 24, 35, 107, 112, 115, 132, 143–5, 147, 149–51, 159
Plotnik, Joshua, 56
Pluhar, Evelyn B, 84, 110

Povinelli, Daniel J., 61, 62
preferences, 3, 8–17, 19–21, 24, 37, 44, 60, 71, 74, 75, 78, 79, 83, 88–92, 98, 105, 106, 109, 137, 139, 146
proto-moral, 30
Psarakos, Suchi, 56

Q

qualia, 42, 51

R

Rachels, James, 79, 80
rationality
  biological, 17
  instrumental, 21, 22
  minimal, 17, 19, 20
  practical, 8, 16, 19, 149, 156
  reflective, 8
reasons, 2–5, 7–9, 12–15, 17–23, 27–30, 33, 35, 37, 44, 62, 64, 66, 71–3, 75, 77, 79–82, 85, 86, 89, 94, 97, 100, 105, 108, 109, 114, 115, 121, 124, 125, 130, 133, 134, 136, 139–41, 144, 147–9, 152, 155, 157, 158
reciprocity, 29, 31
Regan, Tom, 5, 76, 98, 106–14
Reiss, Diana, 56
representations
  internal, 12, 15
  media, 160, 161
  mental, 12, 18, 19, 23–5, 44, 49, 53, 74, 135

Richards, David, 74
Rogers, Lesley J., 39, 79
Rollin, Bernard, 5, 98, 115–20
Rowlands, Mark, 15, 33
Ruddick, William, 74

S

Saidel, Eric, 23
Sandler, Ronald L., 158
self
  abstract, 14, 49, 83, 87, 121–5, 138, 152
  authentic, 69, 70, 72, 76, 81
  awareness, 1, 4, 30, 38, 41, 47, 50, 54, 58, 60, 64, 91, 115, 116, 123, 137, 141
  bodily, 9, 38, 44
  bodyness, 4, 40, 41, 43, 58
  -cognizance, 39, 40
  concept, 52, 61, 62, 145, 146, 149–51
  consciousness, 19, 38–49, 91, 135, 136, 146–8
  core sense of, 42, 54
  directedness, 79
  ecological, 49–55
  explicit sense of, 19, 39
  extended, 52, 53, 121
  government, 80–2, 88, 141, 148
  identity, 4, 42, 61
  I-ness, 39, 40, 49, 52, 61
  interpersonal, 52, 71
  knowledge, 52, 71
  mineness, 4, 40–3, 58, 61, 146
  mirror self-recognition tests, 31, 39, 61, 78, 146
  vs Other, 121

perceptual, 15, 40, 47, 52, 60
phenomenal, 40, 91
prereflective, 53, 111
as prescriptive, 33, 47, 48
private, 45, 52, 53
-referencing, 40
sense of, 9, 19, 29, 32, 41–3, 53, 54, 61, 78, 82
selfhood
  minimal, 58, 111, 119, 120, 145–7, 149
  rich, 88
sentience, 40, 48, 78, 99, 100
Seyfarth, Robert M.
Sherman, P. W., 39, 40
Singer, Peter, 5, 48, 98–106
skepticism, 41, 55
Skidmore, J., 131, 132, 139
speciesism, 86, 99
subjectivity
  animal, 47, 161
subject-of-a-life, 107, 108, 110, 111

T

Teleology, telos, 115, 117–20, 126
theory
  evolutionary, 30, 49, 115

Kantian, 6, 129, 130, 134
of mind, 40, 41, 45, 47, 61, 62, 78, 80, 82

U

utilitarian, calculus, 102, 105, 116

V

value
  inherent, 106–14
  intrinsic, 116, 117

W

Waller, Bruce, 87
White, Thomas, 60, 87
Will, sense of, 54
Wise, Steven M., 77
Wood, Allen W., 138–40
Wright, William, 133

Z

Zahavi, Dan, 1, 41, 42, 52
Zamir, Tzachi, 120
Zhanna, Reznikova, 57

Printed in the United States
by Baker & Taylor Publisher Services